Praise for *The Improvisation Edge*

"My team felt bonded by these improv techniques, and the outcomes were fantastic. I'm a huge fan."
—**Mark Fetting, Chairman and CEO, Legg Mason**

"This book is full of usable skills and real case studies—it demonstrates that Karen Hough's theories are grounded in experience and that corporations can benefit from taking an improvisational approach to better business behaviors. You will recognize scenarios from your own workplace and come away with better ideas for managing your team."
—**Fiona Scott Morton, Professor of Economics, Yale University School of Management**

"This is not your ordinary business book! It's brilliant, cutting-edge, and highly entertaining. If you're looking for a fresh approach to succeeding at work, Karen Hough reveals secrets from the world of improvisation that are worth a million!"
—**Barbara Stanny, bestselling author of *Secrets of Six-Figure Women***

"Improvisation isn't just key to the comedy business—it can be a key to *any* business. Karen brings classic improv principles to the world of business with great intelligence and humor. Should you read her book? Yes, and..."
—**Steve Bodow, Co-Executive Producer and former head writer, *The Daily Show with Jon Stewart*, and seven-time Emmy Award winner**

"Karen Hough does an amazing job of explaining how to translate the energy and creativity of an improv troupe from the stage to the workplace. The result is a set of concise keys that will help build trust and promote collaboration and teamwork within a business environment. The impact is both practical and powerful, not to mention fun."
—**Jerry Stritzke, President and Chief Operating Officer, Coach**

"Karen's improvisational approach is innovative and trendsetting. I am responsible for the development of 60,000 leaders at US Bank and have not seen any approach that provides a better context for individual, team, and organizational development. Truly...Karen creates an environment for others to authentically self discover th~~~ ~~~
strengths and areas of opportunity."
—**Sonny Randall, Leadership Developn**
   President, Central Ohio Chapter, AST

The Improvisation Edge

The Improvisation Edge

Secrets to Building Trust and
Radical Collaboration at Work

Karen Hough

BK

Berrett–Koehler Publishers, Inc.
San Francisco
a BK Business book

Berrett-Koehler Publishers, Inc.

235 Montgomery Street, Suite 650, San Francisco, CA 94104-2916

Tel: (415) 288-0260   Fax: (415) 362-2512   www.bkconnection.com

ORDERING INFORMATION

QUANTITY SALES. Special discounts are available on quantity purchases by corporations,
associations, and others. For details, contact the "Special Sales Department" at the Berrett-
Koehler address above.

INDIVIDUAL SALES. Berrett-Koehler publications are available through most bookstores.
They can also be ordered directly from Berrett-Koehler: Tel: (800) 929-2929; Fax: (802)
864-7626; www.bkconnection.com

ORDERS FOR COLLEGE TEXTBOOK/COURSE ADOPTION USE. Please contact Berrett-Koehler:
Tel: (800) 929-2929; Fax: (802) 864-7626.

ORDERS BY U.S. TRADE BOOKSTORES AND WHOLESALERS.
Please contact Ingram Publisher Services, Tel: (800) 509-4887; Fax: (800) 838-1149; E-mail:
customer.service@ingrampublisherservices.com; or visit www.ingrampublisherservices
.com/Ordering for details about electronic ordering.

Berrett-Koehler and the BK logo are registered trademarks of Berrett-Koehler Publishers, Inc.

Printed in the United States of America

Berrett-Koehler books are printed on long-lasting acid-free paper. When it is available, we
choose paper that has been manufactured by environmentally responsible processes. These
may include using trees grown in sustainable forests, incorporating recycled paper, mini-
mizing chlorine in bleaching, or recycling the energy produced at the paper mill.

LIBRARY OF CONGRESS CATALOGING-IN-PUBLICATION DATA

Hough, Karen.

The improvisation edge: secrets to building trust and radical collaboration at work / Karen
Hough.—1st ed.

   p. cm.

Includes bibliographical references and index.

ISBN 978-1-60509-585-1 (pbk.: alk. paper)

1. Teams in the workplace. 2. Organizational behavior. 3. Trust. 4. Creative ability in business. 5. Improvisation (Acting) I. Title.

HD66.H677 2011

658.4'022—dc22

2010043856

First Edition

15 14 13 12 11   10 9 8 7 6 5 4 3 2 1

Project management and design by Valerie Brewster. Copyediting by Todd Manza.
Proofreading by Don Roberts. Index by George Draffan.

Contents

For my two families:

My beloved Todd, Timothy, Kate, and Trey.

And my improv family—the whole extended clan.

Preface

I have an unconventional job. I use improvisation as the catalyst to train and consult with leadership and business teams. We get results. But when you strip away the fancy language in my sales brochure, it all comes down to the fact that I offer an education in trust—creating it, earning it, keeping it.

I certainly never set out to be a trust specialist. During my early years in business, I didn't realize that I was honing my skills for my current work. I worked in the network engineering industry in New York City for six years, and I was able to consistently close high-margin deals and create long-term relationships with my clients. Though I moved to new companies several times, my clients always followed me and continued doing business with me.

Before New York, I was a professional actor and improviser, based in Chicago for eight years. During that time, I had the same conversation with nine different directors. Some version of "It's been a relief to have you in the show. I can trust that you'll be prepared and won't steal focus."

They didn't realize that I was terrified of screwing up or not being seen as a team player, so I overprepared and showed up early and eager.

However, it really came home to me through the eyes of my account manager in a business I now own. Beginning during her first week on the job, she would shake her head at me and say, "I've never been in a meeting where so many high-level executives trusted our word and were excited to play games!" or "I've never watched a team interact like this ensemble. There are no egos, and you all get so much done so quickly."

I could do this, and so could the special people in my ensemble, because we're improvisers. The innate skills, philosophy, and behaviors of improvisation are radically collaborative, and when you are able to adapt and collaborate on such a high level, you intrinsically engender trust. For more than a decade, we've been using the philosophy and exercises of improvisation to create transformative experiences for people in corporations. Adopting an improviser's mindset and behaviors is a radical new way to make yourself and your organization more profitable, innovative, and trusted.

Improvisers must work in an environment of trust. Improvisation, by its nature, is one of the riskiest, most uncertain fields of performance. It requires a group of performers to create a scene, game, or play without a script. We don't really know what our troupe members will say or do from moment to moment, yet we are able to create incredible shows on the fly. Every improviser relies on her partners, her audience, and her own ability to listen and change to create something, under pressure, in every performance.

Basing my life's work on two such different worlds—the corporate setting and the improvisational stage—sounds very unlikely, I know. So how did we connect business and improv?

I learned about improvisational comedy as an undergraduate at Yale, in the Purple Crayon improv troupe. We performed, got other college troupes off the ground, and kept in touch over the summers. I even studied briefly with the legendary Del Close, the father of long-form improvisation.

Through those experiences, I learned the underlying practices of improvisation as well as some things most people don't know about improvisation: Improv has a clear set of guidelines. Improvisers practice and work at their craft like crazy. Improvisers trust their troupe members implicitly. Really brilliant improv is about finding the least obvious, most surprising outcome in any situation.

These improvisational practices became a part of my DNA. I stopped thinking about these skills and just lived them. It never occurred to me that those improv guidelines might have very strong underlying principles—that the secrets of improvisation were also the secrets of high-performing business teams.

After graduation, I lived two unexpected and utterly different lives. My first life was in performance and improv. I had a great career as a professional improviser and actor. I got paid for my work, trained at the Second City Training Center, and even launched a few improv troupes of my own. Commercials and TV paid the bills, but my passion was experimental, edgy, black-box theater. Professional performance also gave me a thick skin and a propensity to see silver linings. When you audition twenty times and come up with only one part, you become very resilient and practiced.

Things kept improving as I persisted, and I had more than seven solid years of constant work. I was really lucky, really driven, and had a good agent. I did over one hundred live productions.

Then I married, moved to New York for my husband's work, and one day, quite suddenly, realized I was done. I was more than ready for something new. I needed a new challenge for both my brain and my happiness. And I really missed my new husband. He worked during the day and I worked six nights a week.

I dialed my agent in the middle of the day and just quit. We both cried a little but I mostly felt excited and scared. Now I would have to plunge into something new.

So my second life was in network engineering. It was the middle of the nineties and the Internet craze. New York had been affectionately dubbed Silicon Alley, and if you could chew gum and walk at the same time, you could probably get a job in technology, with stock options. Plus, I read a book that passionately convinced me that techies really *needed* a people person like me! And what do you know, Merrill Lynch hired me as a short-term consultant on a Year 2000 hardware assessment.

Let's just pause here. Remember, I was a liberal arts–educated actor. I wouldn't have been able to identify a server if it had fallen on me. But you better believe that I crammed and searched the Internet all night before my interview. Then I was completely honest about my limitations. I promised to be passionate and dedicated, I asked a ton of questions, and I used all of my stored-up improv secrets during the interview. They trusted me when I said I would be able to do the job. I got the gig. And I delivered.

That consulting job was followed by intense stints in three different network engineering start-ups over the next six years. One went public, one remained private, and one was acquired. Despite my lack of experience, I got to head up sales and marketing, helped to open regional offices, and worked seventy-hour weeks. It was a crazy, fantastic, sometimes awful, all-consuming business education, and I loved it.

Simultaneously, two of my friends from Yale, Frances Barney and Mike Everett—also liberal arts–educated actor types—were moving up the ladder in banking and administration. We'd cram and study all night and think on our feet during the day. Then we would have overcaffeinated lunches where we described getting through yet another meeting by collaborating rather than telling, or coming up with a solution no one else had considered, or making a mistake in the office that we turned to our advantage.

It became such a consuming subject that Frances wrote a paper on the idea that improvisation could inform better business practices, for an MBA class at the Wharton School. Professor Michael Useem, who has my gratitude to this day, said, "I think this has legs. Why don't you try it out with my class?" Our company, ImprovEdge, was born.

For more than twelve years, we have conducted research and facilitated learning workshops and development programs, using improv as the catalyst. Our research has uncovered four key principles, based on the secrets of improvisation, that can help accelerate your life, your career, your team, and your organization.

This book is all about how the behaviors of improv enable teams to collaborate on a radical level. And the incredible outcome of those behaviors is trust. This book will explore each of these improv secrets and demonstrate how they are directly related to adaptability, improving organizational performance, and building trust.

The introduction, "Your Biggest Problem at Work and the Most Unexpected Solution," examines how our issues at work are tied to the need to collaborate, to be flexible, and most important, to have and engender trust, and will explain how the four secrets of improvisation are the solution.

Chapter one, "The First Secret of Improvisation: Yes! Space," details how positivity and acceptance create deep capabilities for collaboration, innovation, and engagement.

In chapter two, "The Second Secret of Improvisation: Building Blocks," we will look at why *and* is a really big word and how critical it is to get in there and play.

Radical collaboration using the improviser's mind-set is explored in chapter three, "The Third Secret of Improvisation: Team Equity." One of the components of Team Equity is *equity,* not *equality*; great teams are not about equal input but about leveraging the strengths of the team and using individual talents to work toward a goal.

My favorite part of improvisation, and one of the clear markers of successful businesspeople, is the ability to deal with the unexpected. In chapter four, "The Fourth Secret of Improvisation: Oops to Eureka!," we explore how you're OK even if you screw up, and how the unexpected can create advantages. We also look into mind-set and flexible behaviors.

Each chapter also describes three critical components of each secret and shares hands-on behaviors and exercises that enable you to start adopting the improviser's mind-set. The exercises in this book are not just for master improvisers or professional facilitators. They are for you. They are for anyone willing to try something new.

Finally, in "Practice. Then Celebrate!" we remember the critical importance of practicing new behaviors and celebrating success. The secrets of improvisation only work if you put them into practice, and every time you have even the smallest success you must enjoy and celebrate that step.

Each chapter presents research that ties together collaboration, trust, and improv. I hope you'll also enjoy the stories and case studies from real companies that have used improvisational behaviors to build adaptability and trust within their organizations. This book will provide you with hands-on, immediately usable exercises to adopt an improviser's mind-set. I invite you to use this book to transform yourself, your team, and your organization.

Your Biggest Problem at Work and the Most Unexpected Solution

We all want to be successful, effective, happy people. That's probably one of the most common desires in adult humans. We want to contribute in a meaningful way. We want to enjoy our friends, family, and colleagues; make money; and feel good about our work and life. And these are great desires; they keep us striving, keep us motivated and engaged—keep us *living*.

But what about the problems we face in reaching those goals? It sometimes feels as though we're paddling upstream and that the very things we want to enjoy and rely upon—such as good teams and relationships, challenging projects, and a successful career—just aren't coming together.

The surprise I will explore in this book is that our issues and problems aren't actually about spreadsheets. Or cash flow. Or the economy, clients, salespeople, or even the boss. It certainly feels as if those things are the root of all the frustration, worry, and sleepless nights—and they are a part of it, certainly. But the most important factor underlying all of these elements is trust.

That's right, *trust*. And if that seems startling, get ready for an even bigger surprise.

The key to creating trust and success in the workplace is probably the last thing you would ever imagine. It's improvisation.

Improv. Like the club you visited in Chicago. Like *Whose Line Is It Anyway?* on TV. Like good jazz.

Improvisation, along with the skills and behaviors that are the breath and blood of improvisers, is the surest way to start working at a higher level, creating high-performance teams, exhibiting greater leadership behaviors, and building and engendering trust at work.

⁎ The model for management that we have right now is the opera. The conductor of an opera has a very large number of different groups that he has to pull together. The soloists, the chorus, the ballet, the orchestra, all have to come together — but they have a common score. What we are increasingly talking about today are diversified groups that have to write the score while they perform. What you need now is a good jazz group.

PETER DRUCKER[1]

Let's take some time to think a bit more deeply about trust.

The level and amount of trust you feel affect not only your own performance but also the performance and profitability of your entire organization. Trust in yourself, trust in your team, trust in your boss, and trust in your organization.

We build trust over time, through consistency and behaviors that continually show we are collaborative, innovative, and, well, trustworthy. We have to earn trust through our behavior, and that takes work, because trust is seriously low among us right now. We don't trust our banks, we don't trust our politicians, we don't trust our dry cleaner, and we sometimes don't trust ourselves. This is a serious national issue.

People love to invoke the "good old days," in part because there seems something innocent and rosy about the period one hundred years ago. People then believed that a man's word was his bond. There seemed to be fewer reasons to doubt certain institutions. But then scandals arose, individuals lied, and governments broke their own laws. So now, when we desperately want to just live, to just get through our days, we feel compelled to double check everything: check another newswire, check another reference, check to see if we got enough change back. It's exhausting, time consuming, and saddening, and when we do decide to trust someone or something as a matter of principle, we walk away worrying "Will I be glad or made a fool?"

One of the biggest holes in our ability to trust has to do with our teams and organizations. When we don't trust our colleagues or don't believe that our company has our best interests in mind, we end up without foundational trust. Corporate confidence is at an all-time low as a result of a long wave of shameful activities: Enron's ethical morass, Madoff's lies, Wall Street's collapse, GM's bailout, and the list goes on. It has made us cautious, sad, and slow to trust.

The irony here is that the financial collapse came out of *too much* trust. Most people do not understand the complexities of finance and real estate, so we trusted our financial and real estate institutions and the individuals doing the work to be ethical. We trusted that they would work in a collaborative way that would take into account the greater needs of the market and the country, always looking for a way for everyone to come out ahead. Instead, they acted only on their own behalf, did not collaborate with other entities, and lost track of the big picture.

I've encountered some people who doubt the critical importance of collaborative behaviors. Over the twenty years I've been doing my work, a lot of people have tried to convince me that, professionally, trust shouldn't matter.

"Plow through! If you're a professional, it shouldn't matter if you like or trust other people! Just get it done!" I've actually heard those words come out of a manager's mouth. I doubt his team enjoyed working for him.

When trust is low, people experience stress, which seriously affects our health, mental capabilities, and emotional stability. Daniel Goleman, the researcher behind the concept of emotional intelligence, tells us "stress makes people stupid." He states that people cannot "remember, attend, learn, or make decisions" when they are emotionally upset—when they're worried, frustrated, angry, or hurt.[2]

Have you ever felt any of those emotions at work? The experience of emotional stress creates physical side effects such as higher blood pressure, stomach and intestinal issues, headaches, weight gain or loss, and lower metabolism. We also suffer mentally. We more easily lose control of our temper, we can't prioritize as well, we lose our ability to process rationally, and our memory does not work as well.

All of these emotional and physical side effects result from the stress generated by any environment that keeps us from working together effectively. When people are constantly wondering whether they can share information, if they have to watch their backs, or if their colleagues don't value them, the result is low trust.

Conversely, when trust *is* in place, it creates incredible strength in individuals, teams, and organizations. Relationships stay strong in an atmosphere of respect. Teams overperform when they collaborate and trust that everyone is working toward a common goal. Leaders motivate when followers trust that those leaders are competent and ethical. Organizations thrive when there is trust in the adherence to goals and values. And for that matter, customers buy products because they trust the quality of a brand name. Planes take off because pilots trust that the engineers, air traffic controllers, and ground technicians have done their jobs. And we stay in relationships when we trust that we will be cared for.

As Patricia Aburdene wrote in *Megatrends 2010*, "Transcendent values like trust and integrity literally translate into revenue, profits, and prosperity."[3]

Radical collaboration creates trust. And trust is the key to relationships, teamwork, leadership, and success. So how do we create trust, engage in trustworthy behaviors, and start to reap those personal and professional benefits?

The Most Unexpected Solution You'd Ever Guess

Improvisers step onstage without a script, set, costumes, makeup, or props. They arrive without any of those common tools of theater—and yet, they perform. They create scenes, relationships, comedy, even complete one-act plays on the fly.

Great improv is a lot like deep trust. There's an overwhelming misconception that trust is something that either exists in a relationship or doesn't, that it can't be learned, changed, or built. In the same way, many people believe that improvisers must be born with a special set of skills—skills that either you have or you don't.

Another type of improvisation occurs in jazz. Improv is the departure of a musician from the written music. Imagine that a jazz group is playing a song it has rehearsed and then the saxophone player suddenly begins a solo that's never been written, that she's never played before, and that the rest of her group have never heard. She's creating something entirely in the moment, based on the energy of the room and her own inspiration. Her band members are going with it, listening and contributing a bass line, a riff on the piano, or a faster snare beat based on what they hear from the soloist. At the time, none of them knows how long the solo will go, how much they'll contribute, or if it will turn into a duet. They make it all happen in the moment.

That's improvisation.

Considering that the number one adult fear is public speaking, even when delivering a *prepared* speech, improvisation may sound to some people like a personal horror movie.

"That's impossible," you're thinking. "I don't think anyone could do that. Besides, this is an utterly foreign concept to me. I can't improvise! How could improv possibly make a difference at work?"

But guess what. You *do* improvise. Every single day. Although a quick wit and sense of humor help professional improvisers enormously, they don't have unreachable skills that no one else can learn. As a matter of fact, just like any profession, improvisation has a process, a set of skills, and guidelines for success.

When your boss calls you into her office and asks you to work on a project you've never heard about, one that sounds completely scary, and you say, "Sure, I'd be happy to work on that," you're improvising.

When you're presenting to a big client and she asks a question you've never considered, and you nod and start to answer, then get some support from your partner in the room, you're improvising.

When a critical team member is out sick and you're covering his work while finishing your own, all while pitching in on a surprise proposal that unexpectedly came through the door, you're improvising.

Anyone can improvise, and anyone can learn to collaborate on an extreme level. Improvisers collaborate radically—their level of trust and the intensity of their work are far above and beyond normal teamwork. That sort of behavior is the key to building, managing, showing, and engendering trust. Strangely enough, these concepts are intertwined in a surprising way. Improvisational troupes can't perform well without trust, but trust can't occur unless our behaviors and words show that we are trustworthy. This is true of every group of people who interact, especially in work situations. We can't do our work well, collaborate, or grow if we cannot trust that everything from our basic needs to our ideas is in trustworthy hands. Sound like a circle? It can be, and how we choose to behave determines whether the circle spins backward or forward.

Improvisation and the Workplace

Here's a real situation we encountered with a client a few years ago. We got a call to work on a branding initiative. From the outside, it looked like a very straightforward engagement. Two huge banking entities were merging and the joint leadership was smart enough to realize that they wanted a clean new brand and message (rather than the mashed-up combo you normally see after a merger). The brand message was key; it had to identify what the new organization stood for and its value in the market. The company's leaders also realized that if the organization's employees didn't understand and embrace the new identity it could create confusion for the market.

This was a complicated problem, but not a complex one. Atul Gawande is a writer who researches how we get things done. He contends that complicated problems are difficult, but once they're figured out, they can be solved the same way over and over. Like the bank's leaders, we approached this as a complicated problem. Using a brand image, sales models, workshops, charts, and graphs, we could implement a solution that would be applied ubiquitously.

In collaboration with a marketing strategist, we created a workshop to be rolled out to hundreds of people, ranging from the CEO to the administrative assistants, in two different markets. However, after completing the first workshop, we realized this job wasn't going to be about branding at all. We were stopped in our tracks.

The organization's presenting issue, its own diagnosis of its symptoms, was uncertainty about its organizational identity and poor communication. "Presenting issue" is trainer speak for the behavioral issues that block effective work, and the things that people do and say that create conflict and waste time, money, and resources. And this diagnosis was partly right. There were obvious problems in how the people from the two banks were communicating, which was making everyone leery about their postmerger identity.

But the real, deeper problem only made itself apparent after my ensemble arrived. The banking teams did not trust each other. These people were worried, suspicious, and stressed. They lived and worked in two very different cultures and often misunderstood their new colleagues. They had never collaborated or worked together in a way that allowed them to build trust!

This was a complex problem rather than a complicated one. In a complex problem, outcomes are highly uncertain. These people were exhibiting unexpected emotions, reactions, and concerns. They could not be presented with a one-size-fits-all solution; they had to be dealt with as individual, complex people with particular concerns.

This is what we saw: People in the wealth management branch of the company were worried that their new colleagues wouldn't understand how to manage high-net-worth clients and would weaken their high-profile brand. People on the retail end of the business were offended that their new colleagues treated them with disdain when the retail business was actually bringing to the new organization far more reach and product diversification. In addition, these two groups came from very different parts of the United States: the wealth management group from New York City and the retail branch from the Midwest. Each group made jokes, rolled eyes, and expressed frustration with the other group.

For these people, the situation represented quite a vicious circle: poor communication → no collaboration → misunderstanding → low trust → more guarded communication → lower trust. And on it went.

The lack of collaboration and trust within the organization was leading to a terrible waste of resources and loss of time, money, growth, and innovation. The associates needed to collaborate immediately to meet multiple merger deadlines. Misunderstandings led to inappropriate work product, which led to constant revisions, late nights, and frazzled employees.

I worked closely with one woman in New York who told me that she worked from 9 a.m. to midnight every day. She was living in a hotel and hadn't seen her husband in a week because "there's no one else who can do this. I can't trust anyone in the other market to get it done right, and if this work doesn't happen, it would be disastrous to the merger."

At the same time, a man in the Midwest market was spending hours on the phone and in research because "they're not sharing everything we need. It's as if they don't want to work with us. They don't want to trust us! Every time I go back, I get new information. If they would just share it in the first place, I wouldn't be spinning in circles."

In addition, managers were trying to protect their own employees against unavoidable layoffs. Rather than collaborating with their new colleagues, working together to assess the best talent, and creating the right team, they were protecting turf. I spoke to one manager who resented her counterpart in the other city: "We'll both keep our jobs, but she's getting to keep a lot more of her people than I am just because she's working this politically. My people are better, but they're getting laid off because she's pulling strings!"

In the case of the bank merger, my ensemble had to say something. We talked extensively with leadership about reworking this program. We spoke up about the issues we saw, and we asked to address and record merger issues and to allow the participants to brainstorm solutions. They would know more about their regional cultures, would have in-depth solutions from the field, and people would feel ownership of the new brand and culture of the organization.

With our client's OK, we took action. We retooled the debrief points to address the stress these people were feeling, and added specific exercises to teach collaboration and adaptability. The new workshops gave the employees a forum to talk about the merger and tried to give them a place to look at all sides of the issue. Management actively participated. The merger, the activities related to it, and the level of stress had been unexpected. These workshops focused on enabling the participants to have mentally freeing moments in which they could visualize an outcome and brainstorm about the actions needed to get there. Ideas for growth and greater cultural and brand identity were collected from both markets and then shared across the new enterprise to smooth the transition to a single, merged organization.

> ✳ Few things can help an individual more
> than to place responsibility on him, and to
> let him know that you trust him.
>
> BOOKER T. WASHINGTON[4]

And trust slowly began to improve. The understanding generated by the aggregated information enabled the teams to collaborate more efficiently. Their entrance into a merged organization was easier because they applied the behaviors of radical collaboration.

If you are working in a place that feels like that bank before the merger, it's time to flip this paradigm. It's time to change how we work, behave, and communicate, because when people do feel trusted and engage in trustworthy behaviors, they feel good. They feel motivated and they want to contribute not only their best effort but also their discretionary effort. That's when people go above and beyond, by their own choice, putting in extra time and work because they are committed to success, and it makes such a difference for teams and organizations. Those improvisational behaviors build flexibility, collaboration, positivity, and trust.

The Four Secrets of Improvisation

Improvisation works because of certain principles — secrets, really. Improvisers can accomplish amazing things because they understand these secrets, and if we can learn to apply some of those improvisational secrets to life and work, we too can build trust and accomplish amazing things. This book explores four of the most important secrets of improvisation that create trust: Yes! Space, Building Blocks, Team Equity, and Oops to Eureka!.

The concepts are quite simple. *Yes! Space* is a way for us to bring positivity and creativity into the workplace. *Building Blocks* enables us to take something small and build it into something exceptional. *Team Equity* shows us how to leverage the combined power of the people in our organizations. And finally, *Oops to Eureka!* helps us to understand that the unexpected often yields the greatest discoveries.

There are a lot of great books out there that delve deeply into the definition of trust. If you want to tear apart the subject of trust, subdivide trust into types, and get really academic about it, I recommend you check those out.

This book is about learning and practicing new behaviors and ways to communicate that are radically collaborative and that show and build trust. Those behaviors are based on the principles of improvisation. Let's take a close look at how improvisation can inform our ability to collaborate and trust, and why it is so special.

The First Secret of Improvisation

Yes! Space

Imagine . . . You are backstage at a theater, listening to the sound of an excited crowd taking their seats out front. As you stare at the empty stage, you suddenly realize that you have no script, no costume, no props. You look around at the shadowed faces of the other people backstage, and from their nervousness you realize that they also have no idea what's going to happen next. Suddenly, the lights dim in the house and go up onstage. It's your cue. You have to go out!

You're pulled onstage by the motion of the people behind you. One of your troupe members steps up to the lip of the stage and says, "I need a one-word contribution." Someone in the back of the audience shouts, "Vegetables!" The audience laughs mildly and your troupe member accepts it. "Great!

Vegetables is our subject!" He steps back.
Then nothing else happens.

The faces of the audience regard you and
the silence feels crushing. You've got to do
something! So, without a net, you step out
and proclaim, "I feel like a rutabaga!"

The crowd titters, but you don't know what
to say next. Silence stretches out in front of
you and you start to get warm around the
armpits. Before you know it, a hand slaps you
on the shoulder and one of your troupe says,
"Yes, and you look like one, too!"

The crowd laughs . . .

Does this sound like a nightmare? A movie script? A joke?

Actually, it's what happens every night to an improvisational actor. Improvisation is an art form that demands that
a troupe of performers walk onstage in front of an audience
when they literally do not know what is going to happen
next. The troupe onstage asks the audience to supply ideas
for characters, a plotline, a style of music, a current event,
anything. Taking that idea from the audience, the troupe
starts to create a show, play, comedy scene, or game. The
troupe members think entirely on their feet, making it up
as they go along. They really never know, from moment to
moment, what the other troupe members might say or do.
They just have to go with it and make the performance work.

I've spoken to people who have watched improv and can

barely believe it's real. "How do they do that?" they say, or "It's incredible that they can come up with all of that stuff on the fly. It must be a special talent!" or "There has to be a trick."

The truth is, there are a few tricks. But these tricks are actually a solid set of guidelines that make it possible for improvisers to work wonders. They are simple, effective, and impressive. And you, too, can use those guidelines in your work and life to improve performance, collaborate radically, and build trust.

When we adopt the improviser's mind-set and behaviors, we create trust every day, moment by moment, in the workplace. We will dive into the specific definitions, secrets, and behaviors of improvisation that I have seen applied in the workplace for over a decade.

We all improvise, every day. Every time we deal with an unexpected setback in the office or collaborate on a great project with our team, we are using behaviors grounded in improvisation. Wouldn't it be nice to know how to do it well, like the professionals? And while we're improvising, wouldn't it also be incredible if we could build a strong, effective, and supportive network of trust?

To do so, we need to explore the key secrets of improvisation.

In the onstage scene described above, you and your fellow improvisers were a living example of the first secret of improvisation, Yes! Space. A troupe of improvisers can build a game, a scene, or an entire one-act play in the moment because they have agreed to say yes.

The Yes! Space concept allows for endless possibility, and is very easy to accomplish. To fully understand what happens in Yes! Space, let's break it down into components:

  ✳ Say yes

  ✳ Put the critic on hold

  ✳ Make it public

Say Yes

The very action of saying the word *yes* is critical to improvisation. It's also key to building a collaborative space where people believe they can take risks and be creative. Saying yes is an effective tool for both the improv stage and the workplace.

Think about the vegetable scene onstage. As you remember, you were onstage, in the spotlight. There was no question that you had to act, even though there was no plan. You blurted out the first thing that came to you: "I feel like a rutabaga!" Then one of your troupe members joined you in the scene. She immediately agreed with you. She said, "Yes, and you look like one, too." The very first word your troupe member said was yes. You experienced Yes! Space. It's really that simple. Your contribution to the performance, being a rutabaga, was immediately accepted. No assessments, no lifted brow, no devil's advocate. Just "Yes!"

The power of that little word is amazing. By taking the

action to say the word yes you have entered into positive possibilities.

This power of yes is not a new concept, and it is not confined to improvisation. Many modern disciplines have explored the concept of positive power, and they all agree on the transformational power of positivity. Unfortunately, positivity runs counter to our natural propensity to be negative, and it takes work. For example, researchers have discovered that we actually are wired for negativity in our language and culture. Of 558 emotion words in English, 62 percent are negative. And when people are shown photos of bad or good occurrences, we spend a longer time viewing the bad ones.[1]

We have to work harder to learn to use Yes! Space. That might mean getting comfortable with a little discomfort. But the benefits are very much worth the work.

⁂ yes is a world
& in this world of
yes live
(skillfully curled)
all worlds

FROM E. E. CUMMINGS,
"LOVE IS A PLACE"[2]

Getting to Yes is the Harvard Business School study and book on collaborative negotiation.[3] It changed the face of negotiations and opened a new space for both sides to find the best result in a negotiation. The work of these authors overturned the notion that negotiations must be confrontational, difficult events.

Dale Carnegie based his blockbuster *How to Win Friends and Influence People* on the concept that smiling and expressing a genuine curiosity for others can lead to personal success in life and more sales in business.[4] Consistently questioning and seeking to serve the other person's needs builds safe environments and relationships and makes sales. People prefer to give their money to people and organizations they trust.

Stephen Young, the author of *MicroMessaging*, discusses the great effect of microscopic positive behavioral changes.[5] Simply by nodding, making eye contact, or saying a person's name with respect, Young contends, you have the power to influence how others perceive that person. So the act of saying yes in your slightest inflections, and in a public way, can have a gigantic effect on another person's confidence and success.

The concept of appreciative inquiry contends that, rather than seeking to solve problems in a corporate environment, companies need to focus relentlessly on what they're doing *right*. That upon which you focus, grows. Under the power of the growth of the good stuff, the bad stuff will minimize.

The combination of Yes! Space and appreciative inquiry had a great influence on one of the nation's top children's hospitals. In 2008, the hospital was undergoing major changes in both clinical and administrative functions. We created an improvisational engagement that enabled participants from all areas of the hospital to focus on their ultimate goal: better patient outcomes. During times of great change in organizations, we often see consistently negative behaviors and competition. By embracing the improviser's mind-set and behaviors of Yes! Space, this hospital staff was able to approach the change phase positively and collaboratively.

In the improvisational mind-set, any contribution, no matter how ridiculous, is greeted with immediate agreement. As an improviser, I could trust that if I stepped out onstage and shouted, "I'm the queen of Sheba!" all of my troupe members would say, "Yes, you are!" and start treating me like the queen.

By voicing the word *yes*, you are saying yes to possibility. Yes is not a literal commitment, as in "Yes, we will." It is a commitment to considering a possibility, as in "Yes, we could." This means that every idea or contribution is considered valid. No one sneers, shakes her head, or says no the moment an idea pops out of someone's mouth. The improviser's belief that every idea is valid also assumes that every person is valid. Simply because an idea has been contributed, improvisers believe it is imperative to acknowledge its existence and importance by saying yes to both the idea and the person. Saying yes becomes a reflex for improvisers, and it can become a reflex for you.

The particular idea offered may not be the one we pursue. We have simply agreed that it *could* be one we pursue and that we will explore it together. By agreeing to give it a chance to live and breathe, even for two minutes, we have said yes to its possibility.

Saying yes is imperative for improvisation because the performance would never go anywhere if we kept denying ideas. When I shout, "I'm the queen of Sheba," my troupe member could say, "No, that's not a good idea. Let's be mechanics instead. I know all about mechanics but I don't know anything about the queen of Sheba, and neither do you." After that, another troupe member could say, "Mechanics aren't funny. Let's sing a song instead."

Can you imagine how dumb that would look onstage? Time would be wasted, the audience would be confused, and the troupe would not be working as a team, only as individuals out for themselves.

Yes! Space and saying yes means that we are going to get the performance rolling right away. Because there are no preconceived notions about what must happen, as there is in a scripted show, we can accept anything. And by accepting every possibility, at least for a while, the performance moves quickly and efficiently.

What does the say yes reflex mean for everyday encounters? Whenever I work with groups, the event organizers approach me afterward to discuss the high level of engagement: "So many people spoke up! We had people contributing who had never engaged in a training session before! How do you do it?"

I say yes. That's how I do it.

The first word out of my mouth, every time someone contributes, is yes. When that happens, the group learns that it's safe to share. They realize that they won't be criticized or ignored, and suddenly they want to start being a part of the conversation. When I ask open-ended questions, there often are moments of silence until some brave soul decides to fill the silence. When they are greeted with agreement, they feel validated, strong, and they contribute again. Then the people around them start to contribute and soon you have a room full of interacting people.

Try it sometime. You'll be amazed at the exponential increase in engagement.

When we say yes, we're agreeing that others have the right to air their ideas, and we are saying yes to possibility. As the session progresses, we may debate the idea or change to another topic, but we can always agree that a person's contribution was worthwhile by saying yes in that moment. This can be particularly effective when people are struggling or need to share something difficult. By saying yes, we can create a place in which it is safe for everyone to share.

I remember a particular session when my ensemble was working with groups from an insurance company that included call center personnel, managers, and even board members. We had a tight time frame in which to teach a few concepts. One woman who had not spoken up during the entire session responded to our discussion of Yes! Space by saying that she felt ignored by her colleagues and that people never thanked her for her hard work. She was, by nature, a rather gruff person.

I said, "Yes, and that must be hard for you. What more can you tell us about your feelings on this?" She shared that she loved her work and really wanted people to recognize her accomplishments. At that point, other members of the group chimed in and said they would agree to be her sounding board. One man even said, "Yes, I noticed your good work. I'm sorry I never commented on it."

The conversation was cathartic and positive, and in a few

minutes the woman asked me to continue with the exercise, for which she volunteered.

The point here is not so much her response as the response of the in-house trainer after the session. She thanked me for managing the event and then singled out that particular moment in the session.

"I would have been so scared!" she said. "I would have just tried to steer the conversation back to the agenda and not comment on that uncomfortable situation. I would not have wanted to let her keep talking for fear it would become a big issue. I'm so glad you managed it!"

Saying yes does indeed create some risk, but it also creates resolution, as it did for the woman who needed to be heard.

Put the Critic on Hold

Imagine a critic. In my mind, I see a wizened pundit peering over his glasses with a sarcastic sneer. He knows so much more than me. I know he'll discount or even laugh at anything I say. And if he really hates an idea, he'll literally scream, "No!"

Put him on hold. Seriously. Punch the pause button on the video in your brain and stop him in his tracks. This is absolutely necessary to Yes! Space.

Putting the critic on hold addresses how Yes! Space deals with something we want to reject. Saying no is a human defense mechanism. When we are faced with an idea or situation that makes us feel surprised or uncomfortable, it is safer to say no. That way, we will not need to stretch, change, or say or do anything that feels risky or scary. We are trained to be logical, rational, linear thinkers. When I suggest that I am the queen of Sheba, you may first react with logic, reason, or even sarcasm. It is a ridiculous statement and it would be far safer to simply kill the idea than to take part in it.

Putting the critic on hold is the loophole for the logical mind. It's another reflex that teaches your brain to say to itself, "That sounds utterly ridiculous and improbable. However, I am going to stop myself from using negative judgment right now. I'm going to allow my brain to agree that this idea is possible, if only for a little while."

Knowing that evaluation and critique can happen later also allows the critic to relax. The critic in your brain can say, "OK, I really want to speak up now, but I'll lie low until this idea has been fully, positively vetted. Then I'll be better able to judge its merit."

Every time you see a movie featuring aliens, space travel, fictional creatures, or anything you know is not real, your brain puts the critic on hold. For those two hours in the movie theater, we agree to believe the impossible is real. If every time a weird, creative idea arose for a novelist or scriptwriter, his or her colleagues said, "That doesn't exist. Don't do it," we would have no *Star Wars,* no *Lord of the Rings*—no SpongeBob, for that matter.

Let's think about our discerning, professional minds. At school and at work, we're evaluated on how critically we can think. We like to ask questions such as "Where are the problems? How can we anticipate all the bad stuff?"

If you are handed a document to review, the first thing you look for is typos, bad grammar, loose content, and you send it back full of red ink and comments on what was wrong. If your significant other or child comes up with a crazy idea for the weekend that doesn't immediately appeal to you, you probably try to introduce doubt. And during meetings, if someone goes off the agenda with a new idea or suggestion, we inwardly seethe. When a new employee throws out a suggestion, it is often met with any number of the following responses:

"I don't know about that."

"We tried it two years ago and it tanked."

"Good idea. But it will never work."

When the critic moves into our relationships with people, we shut down contribution, ideas, trust, and Yes! Space.

You may be thinking, "I'm a lawyer; I have to say no sometimes." Or "I'm a parent. For the safety of my children, I have to say no sometimes!" You're right. You do. This is where theory meets practical application. Yes! Space does work onstage, but even improvisers sometimes introduce no for the sake of comedy. If that scene with the vegetables had gone on for a while and then had become boring or was getting no reaction from the audience, believe me, a good improv troupe definitely would have switched gears. The troupe would give the idea space to grow, to be tested, but if it wasn't going to work, they'd realign for the sake of the show.

Sometimes, we just have to say no. One great way to begin getting used to Yes! Space is to learn to say no in the

Yes! Space. My ensemble and I facilitate an activity about finding different ways to say no and involving another person in the solution. It opens new avenues for everything from effective negotiations to better client interactions. It teaches you to communicate in a way that brings people into collaboration rather than conflict. The key is to ask open-ended questions about what someone really wants and about their needs and motivations.

The next time you want to just say no, try to do it without using the words *no, but, if, however* or any negative contraction such as *can't, won't, don't, shouldn't,* and so forth. It will be tough and frustrating at first. We often fall back on telling or demanding, relying on negative words. But if we first seek to understand, some surprising things can arise.

Question, question, question. Use phrases like "Help me understand" and "Tell me more about your ideas behind this." You may discover a middle ground to replace the no, and the person you're speaking with may realize that the best answer is no without you ever having to say so.

I worked with a marketing manager at a large national bank who had been an improviser in college, and she related a funny story during our session. When she married, she told her husband all about the secrets of improv. However, he started holding her accountable to those principles. Whenever they had an argument, he would smile and say, "You're denying me! You're not saying yes!"

The whole group cracked up at her story, and we went on to talk about how saying yes does actually work in conflictive situations. Her husband was reminding her that, although they had different opinions, she had to remember to honor his, listen to his, and consider the possibility of accepting his. He understood that he might not get his way, but he was asking for the conflict to be positive in nature.

Putting the critic on hold is a way to quicken the pace of collaboration. Think about the vegetable scene again. You are onstage in front of an audience that is expecting a performance right now! You didn't know they would suggest vegetables, and it surprised you. You'd certainly rather pick a subject that you know more about or think might be easier to use as a comic foundation. You are feeling pretty uncomfortable already, but something has to happen. If you don't do something with your troupe now, the entire show, all the money invested in the venue and rehearsals, lights and attendants, will go out the window. The audience will demand its money back, bad reviews will circulate about your lack of professionalism, and the theater could close. By not falling prey to the critic, you can get the show rolling immediately.

Putting the critic on hold is one of the toughest demands of Yes! Space. It requires adjusting and changing your mind, your opinion, and your actions. It can be difficult even for trained improvisers, because the unexpected can really surprise and throw a person off.

I've been surprised many times onstage when a troupe member introduced something I didn't expect or like. But I know I have to adjust and keep the reality working onstage. Maybe I'm pantomiming digging a hole but my troupe member looks at my movements and interprets something

else. She says, "Rowing a boat can be such good exercise."
I want to feel mad that she misinterpreted my intentions; I
want to take control of the scene. But in Yes! Space I've got
to put my critic on hold. I've got to dump my idea and jus-
tify the fact that we are now in a boat.

In real-life situations, I've struggled with this part of Yes!
Space. When someone tells me something I don't agree
with, my improviser's reflex pushes me to say, "Yes!" But
then I pause, because even though I've followed through on
the first aspect of Yes! Space (saying yes), my brain needs
time to adjust to the new reality and to put my critic on hold.
I have to think to myself, "OK, I didn't expect that idea and
I don't like it right off the bat. However, it is valid, and this
person deserves the chance to air the idea with someone
who will support it in a positive way." After I've quieted the
screaming critic, I can keep moving forward. The critic will
have her chance to speak later.

It's interesting to note that following through on these
concepts is easier at work or onstage than at home. I've
always believed that if you can put a management or inter-
personal concept to the test at home, you can make it work
anywhere. For instance, I once returned from conducting a
workshop focused on Yes! Space when my daughter, Kate,
who was four years old at the time, had a friend over. The
kids were happily engaged in the basement and as I cooked
dinner I noticed out of the corner of my eye that Kate was
running up and down the stairs. First she changed into her
bathing suit, and then she was carrying different toys down
from her room. I heard laughing and felt confident that all

was well. Then, about twenty minutes later, Kate's friend came up and announced, "Kate is pouring buckets of water into the playroom. Is that OK?"

I ran down to discover about an inch and a half of standing water in our slightly sunken basement playroom. In my greatest moment of self-control ever, I put my critic on hold. The critic wanted to scream, "What are you doing?! You've ruined our basement and your toys! Get to your room right now! *Time out!*"

Instead, I tried to think about the lessons I had just been espousing and I said, "Kate, darling, can you help me understand why you poured water into your playroom?" And my little girl said, "Oh, Mommy, remember yesterday you said you were so tired of winter and missed the pool? See, I made a pool right here, and we can go swimming soon and you'll be happy!"

I'm so glad I didn't let the critic speak first. Granted, it was a terrible cleanup job, but Kate and I did it together and we both learned a few things that afternoon. I learned that understanding underlying motivations is key to building relationships, and she learned that water does not work everywhere.

Make It Public

The last and most powerful way to create Yes! Space is to make it public. By entering Yes! Space with at least one other person, the event becomes public. However, it also involves some risk, because it forces us to take action on our positive intentions. We may want to support others' actions or ideas, but until we publicly engage, we have not shared that power.

Yes! Space *can* be an individual activity. We can have immediate positive thoughts, say yes to occurrences and unexpected events in our lives, and put the critic on hold in the case of our own ideas and what we see and hear. However, Yes! Space in its truest improvisational sense is a team experience. We engage and risk together, and when we involve even one other person we make it public.

There's a very simple wrap-up game my ensemble plays in our workshops. We stand in a circle. One person turns to the person on his or her right. The two people make eye contact, raise their fists in the air, and shout "Yes!" simultaneously. Then the second person turns to the right, makes eye contact with a new person, and together they shout "Yes!" The yes goes all the way around the circle, speeding up and gaining volume as it goes. The people laugh and watch, anticipating the moment they'll join the yes circle as well. At the end, we all shout "Yes!" one last time together, facing the middle and watching one another.

When I ask participants "Where is the Yes! Space in this game?" they move to the middle of the circle. The entire environment, the whole room and all of us in it, is part of the Yes! Space. We just created it. By paying it forward and giving the yes to each member of the group, we created organizational Yes! Space. We have made it completely public and involved everyone in the room.

This game is a metaphor for the energy and benefit of Yes! Space in an organization. When we make it public, we are not only sharing; we are also reflecting the positivity in ourselves. Making Yes! Space public supports the idea of a place where ideas are heard. When people feel that they are heard, that their ideas are considered and vetted, they want to continue to contribute. Public yes is elemental in creating a trusting, positive, and innovative environment.

I once worked with the CEO of a biopharmaceutical research company. He shared with me that he sometimes hesitated to compliment his direct reports. "I don't want to be seen as playing favorites. I demand a lot from all of my direct reports, and I want to be fair."

I talked to him about making it public and about the fact that support, when made public, actually benefits everyone. Keeping silent to be "fair" actually withholds important feedback that people need to hear. We worked on ways that he could mention and compliment exceptional effort whenever he saw it. We soon found that when behaviors were illuminated and commented upon by this important leader, everyone began to engage in more exceptional behaviors. There was a greater environment of trust and those direct reports, in turn, began to support their own reports more vocally.

The act of making it public also is the cornerstone of organizational transformation. There is no way that new concepts and behaviors can be repeated and their trust benefits reaped until there is visibility. Everyone needs to start doing and saying. After teams begin to publicly see each other saying yes and putting the critic on hold, they in turn will exhibit those behaviors.

It's just so easy. Walk through these three steps the next time someone says, "I have a crazy idea": say yes, put the critic on hold, and make it public.

You'll be standing in Yes! Space.

How Yes! Space Applies to Business

In our example vegetable scene onstage, the improv troupe and the audience have decided that vegetables will be the topic for the show. Think about that. A roomful of people have decided that they are willing to watch a performance about vegetables. Vegetables! The most hated word in a four-year-old's vocabulary. A subject for nutrition, not performance. Yet here we all are, saying yes to this crazy idea. In the interest of comedy, we are willing to suspend our penchant for results, logic, and reason. The question is, how is that important to our actual lives?

How would it feel to have the entire office shout "Yes!" after all of your suggestions? Probably unreal, like you're in a funny commercial. Or wry, like you're in the classic scene from *When Harry Met Sally*. Or maybe great?

It might make you want to contribute again. It might make you feel like a creative, intelligent person.

My company has an exercise in which volunteers brainstorm about a crazy idea and the entire room responds by shouting "Yes!" after every idea, no matter how unusual. I've facilitated this exercise over three hundred times and the volunteers always comment on how energized they felt, how smart they felt, how the flow of ideas sped up as the exercise progressed.

The people in the audience always comment on how much they wanted to jump in with their ideas, how fun it was to watch and shout "Yes!" along with the volunteers. And in almost every session, an audience member will say,

"At the beginning, I was so glad I didn't volunteer to stand up there. Yet, by the middle of the exercise, I was wishing I could play, too." As the exercise progresses, people want to contribute, they want to be part of the solution, they want to be a leader.

Doesn't that sound like an employee or colleague you'd like to have? Because the format of the game demands that all contributions be greeted with yes, volunteers can trust that they will not be criticized, no matter what happens. They enjoy all three aspects of Yes! Space: their team says yes to every idea, all critics are put on hold because no evaluation or critique is allowed, and the Yes! Space is made entirely public because the brainstorming and responses are done together. In the space of a simple improv game, Yes! Space and very high levels of trust are built.

Here's the tough part: For years, I've been conducting an informal survey after the yes game. In every group I facilitate, I ask the participants how many times in their professional career they've had someone support them as strongly as we did in this exercise. How many times has a manager or colleague smiled, slapped you on the back, or exclaimed, "Wow! That was a great idea! Yes!"?

In over three hundred sessions, with anywhere from fifteen to one hundred participants in the room, I've had exactly three people say they had experienced a strong yes at work. Three people.

One of the three people was a woman who said a boss had been so thrilled by her idea that he hooted "Yahoo!" right outside her cubicle, then told everyone that she had thought of a great cost-saving initiative. She was so energized and thrilled by it that she realized she wanted to contribute even more to her team. She found herself arriving at work early and diving in with gusto for almost a month. It made her feel valued, smart.

If you are a leader or manager, it's time to assess the effect of your communication on the morale of your team. Count the number of times in the past week you have told peers, reports, or colleagues that their idea was extraordinary or their contribution valued. When do you say yes? Are you setting a public example of Yes! Space?

Albert Schweitzer once said, "Example is not the main thing in influencing others. It is the only thing." People learn and change by seeing others do. By saying yes to ideas and contributions, just long enough to enable them to breathe and live for a while, you take a break from the critic ruling your interactions, and your positive example creates safety, trust, and collaboration among your team.

Unfortunately, according to my informal survey, Yes! Space is an exception rather than a rule. Everyone wants engaged employees who care, who give discretionary effort, who go above and beyond. Lots of time and money is spent surveying and defining how engaged we and our associates are and how we might improve performance. Can it really be as simple as saying yes?

A 2001 paper from the Consortium for Research on Emotional Intelligence in Organizations found that for every 1 percent improvement in the service climate (a company in a good mood), there's a 2 percent increase in revenue.[6] This study, conducted by Benjamin Schneider at the University of Maryland, looked at banks, insurance companies, call centers, and hospitals. Can you believe that? By simply raising the mood, positive encouragement, and emotional stability of your team by 1 percent, you can increase your revenues by 2 percent.

So, if you took a little time to say yes, put the critic on hold, and make it public, what could that accomplish? It could make your associates feel heard and valuable. It could create a sense of stability, confidence, and well-being across the office environment. It could improve your bottom line. Could any of us do that tomorrow, or even today? The answer is yes!

Another study, conducted by HealthStream Research, found that improving the relationship between managers and employees, and inserting positivity and recognition of achievement, reduced turnover at a major health-care system from 32.5 percent to 12.7 percent in just three years.[7] Management started to say thank you (which is another way of saying yes to a contribution). They put their critics on hold and looked for the best in people rather than the worst. And they made it public by giving those people rewards and recognition for their achievements.

A Yes! Space Place

We work with one of the largest scientific organizations on the globe, and this organization is the first and only corporate setting where our yes game was received with complete understanding. As a matter of fact, in piloting a new training, the stakeholders told us that saying yes, accepting new and crazy ideas, was an ingrained part of their culture. They were old pros at saying yes, putting the critic on hold, and making it public. Therefore, they wanted to delve into a different aspect of improv.

When I asked about this part of their culture, I was told with a smile, "It's our mission to be great scientists and innovators. It's what we bring to our clients. If we were to be so arrogant as to mistrust a weird idea, or not give our people space to explore in a positive environment, we'd never be where we are today." An improviser's yes is exactly the same yes my client uses with its researchers. It encourages their best and brightest to run with new ideas and concepts.

That conversation felt so good, it was like being back onstage with my favorite improv ensemble. I was among friends. Consequently, my company went on to do very cutting-edge work with this scientific client over several years. Their sensibility for Yes! Space allowed us to take great risk and to enjoy great reward in our client-consultant relationship.

Now let me share what several of my other clients and friends said before we began working with this organization:

"Good luck with that one. Scientists are so linear; they'll never get your stuff."

"Are you kidding? You're working with them? I doubt the improv thing will go well over there."

"There's no chance those rocket scientists will want to step outside the box."

Sometimes I wonder how many people have been talked out of great accomplishments, great relationships, or great adventure because they couldn't get a simple yes.

Let's take a look at how another company used Yes! Space

to accelerate its business process. It was a simple change, a small change, and the benefits have been huge.

Yes! Space Case Study: NBBJ

NBBJ is a global architecture firm whose vision is to shape a future that enhances life and inspires human potential and spirit through design. Its U.S. division, Studio 20, engaged ImprovEdge over a number of years to lead team retreats and long-term leadership development programs for its architects, designers, and administrators.

The idea of Yes! Space, with its energy, humor, and power, really appealed to the studio's personnel. They are a collection of incredibly intelligent, creative people, and their grasp of the components of Yes! Space was impressive. They were able to immediately embrace the behaviors of saying yes, putting the critic on hold, and making it public. In fact, it became common language within the studio: "I need a little Yes! Space in this conversation" or "My critic is screaming. Could you help me put it on hold?" or "I need to make it public and bounce around some ideas. Can you share some Yes! Space with me?"

Saying Yes at NBBJ

One of NBBJ's Studio 20 core team members realized that the organization had an issue with its charrettes. A charrette is a public forum for an architect or designer to show his or her new work. Picture boards are displayed and people walk around looking at the designs and making comments. It's a key part of the process of reaching both client and design goals.

This NBBJ leader had noticed that the architect or designer whose work was displayed often was silent for most of the charrette. He also began to notice that, following a charrette, the designer would return with work that had been totally redone, rather than preserving initial strengths and just fixing weaknesses. He watched and realized that, in the course of a charrette, 90 percent of the comments from attendees comprised criticism or suggestions for change. The architect or designer wasn't hearing about what he or she had done right!

It's an unfortunate assumption: we believe that if we don't comment on positive details a person will automatically understand that those parts are fine. However, after taking such a beating, the architect or designer often went back and changed everything, feeling he or she had been a failure.

The leader realized that the organization needed to mindfully create some Yes! Space. He decided to say yes to recognizing the issue: yes, there is something that we can change here.

Putting the Critic on Hold at NBBJ

The core team leader approached his colleagues and described what he saw. He made his concerns public. It was a little difficult for them to hear at first. Charrettes are an important part of their work, and the setup and process were quite ingrained. However, they put their critics on hold and realized exactly what they needed to do for their designers, who were suffering from a surfeit of criticism. Basically, the entire studio needed to put its critics on hold for the good of progress, design, and employee engagement. The studio's leaders entered into a collaborative conversation and came up with a solution.

Making It Public at NBBJ

Through executive collaboration, followed by all-studio collaboration, Studio 20 agreed to invoke an initial period of Yes! Space at the beginning of every charrette. Reviewers were asked to put their critic on hold and first to speak publicly about what they liked, the strengths, and the positive aspects of a design. This Yes! Space is a highly public exchange of support, encouragement, and focus on design strengths. The new process has built trust and communication within the team, and designs now move forward at a faster rate. Collaboration has improved, and the team has even introduced the concept of Yes! Space into its client meetings. Entire projects move forward faster.

All it took was a simple change. Just a few minutes of behaving like improvisers up front and then entire projects move forward more quickly and efficiently. So many people think that change has to be uncomfortable, time consuming, and difficult, but all it took at NBBJ was ten minutes of group Yes! Space. They have saved hours of designer time, thousands of dollars of wasted effort, and have avoided many disappointed designers and clients.

Yes! Space Behaviors

It's time to think about the most basic behaviors we can put into place to practice Yes! Space. These are simple things you can do right now, today, to bring positivity to work.

* **Say yes.**
  Practice the reflex of responding with the word *yes* after contributions: "Yes, John. Tell me more about that."

* **Put the critic on hold.**
  Slow down and temporarily suspend judgment. Listen to conversations and stay with the speaker. Don't let your predispositions decide your response or take you out of the moment. If you don't like something you hear, just say yes and keep nodding and listening. Try to do it just once today.

* **Make it public.**
  If you like someone's work, tell them. If they exceed expectations, tell the team. If they make a superstar move, tell the organization.

It worked for NBBJ and it can work for you. The following exercise is another great way to bring Yes! Space into your everyday work.

Yes! Space Exercise

Fabulous Conference Calls[8]

Conference calls can be a great tool. Unfortunately, we know how common it is to multitask during a call—put it on mute, leave the room, write an e-mail. So, how can we make conference calls more useful? It can be especially tough when you are the one in charge of organizing or leading conference calls.

In this activity, you get to share the responsibility for the call. Participants will feel accountable and respected, and they'll see just how worthwhile the call really can be. Better yet, they may even stop checking e-mail.

Get Ready

1. Invite as few participants as possible. The fewer the people, the easier it is to engage everyone.

2. Engage the senses. Send something tactile through the mail for participants to hold. Or send a piece of candy to eat. Paint a picture with words. Use colors, describe things graphically, tell stories.

Get Set

3. Divide the agenda into parts and send a section to each team member. Brief them, give them time to prepare, then have them take ownership of that section. Remember, if 90 percent of your contribution is questions, then 90 percent of the call will be others talking.

4. Prepare a list of participants so that, during the call, you can call everyone by name and ask them to comment.

Go

5. At the beginning of the call, have everyone share something from work that recently has gone well. At the end of the call, have everyone commit to take an action based on the call.

6. Use Yes! Space. Whenever someone contributes, even in the slightest way, thank them, support them, respond positively. They will continue to contribute.

Chapter Two

The Second Secret of Improvisation

 *Building Blocks*

So, without a net, you step out and proclaim, "I feel like a rutabaga!"

The crowd titters, but you don't know what to say next. Silence stretches out in front of you and you start to get warm around the armpits. Before you know it, a hand slaps you on the shoulder and one of your troupe says, "Yes, and you look like one, too!" The crowd laughs loudly, and she adds, "Now, I happen to prefer tomatoes for a date, but a rutabaga should mix it up a little."

Four more members of your troupe leap out in front of you, making a small table and two chairs with their bodies. You both "sit" and a fifth person steps up with his arm crooked and says in a French accent, "And may I take your order, Monsieur Rutabaga and Mademoiselle Boston Lettuce?"

> Mademoiselle Boston Lettuce hums over a "menu" suddenly supplied by the hand of her "chair," which has reached around to give her something to read. She exclaims, "Yes! And I'll have the photosynthesis shake with a side of good topsoil . . ."

You're back onstage!

In this scene, your improv troupe has just employed the second critical improvisational principle, Building Blocks. How do you know Building Blocks is being used onstage? Because of the word *and*.

Why *and* Is a Really Big Word

And—that one little word is the foundation for building an entire performance. It always follows a yes in improv. Therefore, the combined power of Yes! Space and Building Blocks is contained in the simple phrase "Yes, and . . ."

This is the biggest secret to improv. "Yes, and" is the central core, the brains of the organization, and the catalyst for the experiment. It's the reason improv works.

Let's think about how the word *and* pumps up the activity. The Building Blocks concept breaks down into three simple steps:

* Jump in and play

* Shelve your ego

＊ Bring a block

These three behaviors are the how-to of Building Blocks. From nothing, improv troupes build huge performances, simply by bringing in the behaviors of Building Blocks.

The concept is best explained if you think about an exercise we use with our clients that is actually called Building Blocks. It's a thought-generating session, which is the inverse of brainstorming. In a brainstorming session, random ideas are tossed out without relation. If every idea in a brainstorming session were a brick, you'd end up with a big, flat field of bricks. That's because in brainstorming, ideas are thrown out in great quantity but without the structural support to help them grow into larger ideas. More than 75 percent of the ideas generated in any brainstorming session usually are discarded without further investigation.

However, when you conduct a session in Building Blocks, and every idea is a brick, you end up with a castle. That's because every idea must relate to or support the original idea in some way. All contributions must expand upon the original idea, see how far it can be stretched, explore it in every possible way. Suddenly, one tiny block of an idea grows into a huge structure we can climb into.

Let's look at the three components of Building Blocks.

Jump In and Play

When you say the word *yes,* you're agreeing to let the other person's idea be valid and to publicly support that person. But when you add the word *and,* you are committing to much more. You're basically jumping into the middle of the game and picking up the ball. You are saying that you are willing to work with others, in the trenches, to make an idea come to life. You are committing your own sweat equity. You are jumping in and playing.

In other words, if *yes* is putting a toe in the water, then *and* is jumping into the lake.

And carries with it the responsibility to contribute. It's not enough to just support the idea or agree with the contribution. For real skin in the game, for real movement, you've got to play too. *And* demands that you jump in, take part, and share the risk and reward. You build with your troupe members, adding blocks and ideas to support their first contribution. When teams know they can trust their colleagues to jump in every time, they can create with incredible courage.

In the vegetable scene, it's not enough just to agree and move on to whatever you would rather do. You have to commit to taking the suggestion of vegetables as far as it will go.

Look at it this way: If your troupe members were to just step up and say, "Yes! You are a rutabaga!," they would be agreeing with you, but it would take the scene no further. They would have no part in the creation and no stake in where it was going. You'd be forced to keep creating alone. Think how ridiculous that would seem.

"I feel like a rutabaga!"

"Yes, you are a rutabaga!"

"Er . . . and you are a Boston lettuce."

"Yes! I'm a Boston lettuce."

"Um . . . and we'll go to a restaurant."

"Yes! We'll . . ."

Bored yet?

The moment your fellow troupe member stepped up, slapped you on the back, and said, "Yes, *and* you look like one, too!," she jumped in and started to play. She committed to sharing the work of creating the scene. Then she took it even further. She created a relationship with your rutabaga ("Now, I happen to prefer tomatoes for a date, but a rutabaga should mix it up a little."). She added a new component to the scene—a dating relationship! She entered the scene in the spirit of play and fun, relaxed and creative, and the whole scene grew. She jumped in with an expectation that this would be positive.

As we examine why improv is such an effective template for better business, I use the word *play* here very intentionally. As a new entrepreneur, I wore dark suits and leaned heavily on my company's decade of extensive research on the underpinnings of improvisation. I spouted statistics and made sure that participants understood the connections to organizational dynamics, psychology, and science. But it was the play, the freedom and the fun, that continued to set our work apart. People at our engagements felt safe to play and discover things about themselves and their colleagues. They left renewed and wanting more, because we were reminding people of the importance of letting go, of jumping in to play.

Dr. Stuart Brown, founder of the National Institute for Play, has spent years looking at the effects of play on our world. He and others in his field have discovered that play is necessary for our success, happiness, and survival. Play occurs not only in mammals but also in life forms at surprisingly low levels. The seemingly unnecessary activity of play is perpetuated despite evolution, which proves its necessity. Play allows us to practice, discover, and experiment.

For example, the tussling of young bears teaches them how to fight and hunt. In the words of Brown's colleague, scholar and play behaviorist Bob Fagen, "In a world continuously presenting unique challenges and ambiguity, play prepares these bears for an evolving planet."[1]

Brown contends that one of the key hallmarks of play is improvisational potential. When we play, "we are open to serendipity, to chance. . . . The act of play itself may be outside 'normal' activities. The result is that we stumble upon new behaviors, thoughts, strategies . . . fresh insights. For example, an artist or engineer at the beach might have new ideas about their work while building a sand castle."[2]

By releasing ourselves to jump in and play, to improvise, we are increasing our ability to be more innovative and effective. When you play with a team, you build trust and collaboration as you give yourself over to the game or activity. People can sense that you've jumped in fully, and they trust that they can play with you.

Plato said, "You can learn more about a person in an hour of play than in a year of conversation." That's because when we play, we truly become ourselves. We tap into our most instinctual responses, and our thoughts and actions quicken.

Over the years, we've worked extensively with a global accounting firm. I've learned that the firm's partners mindfully participate alongside their new associates in our workshops, because those partners have found that they can ascertain much more about the personality and drive of a new associate in our workshop than they ever could in an interview or work setting. Some partners actually cherry-pick from the group, gathering talent for big projects based on how well the individuals play. If someone is enthusiastic, suggesting solutions to challenges, supporting teammates, and just plain having fun, partners take note. Those senior leaders know that during improvisational games they are getting the best measure of those associates' ability to collaborate, because they are relaxed, having fun, and fully engaged. They are showing the truest side of themselves.

Conversely, the leaders also have made judgments about young associates who do not commit to the action, who don't understand how this exercise supports their work, who sneak out their BlackBerrys or let everyone else finish the activity. These participants miss out on the best assignments back at the office.

This accounting firm has an extremely high-performance culture. I've interviewed many of its most successful partners, and a common thread among all of them is their contention that it's been a fun career. *Fun.* It's one of the first words they say when I ask them about their success—often quickly followed by "Some days I can't wait to get to my team and jump in."

Shelve Your Ego

A big part of the success of Building Blocks is believing that group collaboration is better than individual contribution. That's not always easy. When an improviser says "Yes, and," he or she has agreed to follow a troupe member's idea instead of her own. Shelving your ego means letting go of all the good ideas that you are, undoubtedly, in love with. In the vegetable scene, the good of the performance relies on everyone bringing a block that will build on the big idea of vegetables.

For example, our vegetable scene would not work if one person were off by himself acting like a scientist rather than contributing to the idea of vegetables. It would be disconnected and confusing for the audience to watch. However, if that person were a scientist working on his formula for talking vegetables, everything would seem connected. The compounding interest of more and more things contributing to the vegetable idea makes the show much more amusing.

There actually are two sides to shelving your ego. On the one hand is the difficult side: If you show up with the whole castle in your head, built to your specifications, you're really just looking for a yes. You don't want people messing with your blueprints and you don't want their ideas. You just want them to add the bricks that you specify, in the order you feel is correct. Although that feels comfortable and controlled, it also carries a terrible weight of responsibility. It confines the project to the space of one person. Ultimately, it is a terrible waste of the team's brains.

On the other hand, if you do commit to collaboration and give up your blueprints, it can be a terrible blow to watch your castle crumble. Your team may accept only your first block and then take it in a direction you never intended. That can hurt. But this is where the liberating side of shelving your ego can really be an asset. The truth is, you only have to show up with one block. You may not even know where it fits or why you brought it. If your entire team is committed to Building Blocks and to creating the best castle they possibly can, it will all work out.

In improvisation, we often contribute something unknown just to get the action started. I've stepped out and started waving my arms around without the slightest idea what I was doing, or shouted "Linguini!" at the top of my lungs without a plan about where it would go. That's because I was completely secure in the knowledge that my troupe would employ Building Blocks. It was OK that I had not thought everything through. They would help me do that. I completely shelved my ego, let my troupe define what I was doing, and waited to see how their blocks would support mine. For example, in response to my crazy arm movements, a partner might say, "You know, flying by airplane might be a better choice." And after my shout of "Linguini!," three more troupe members might step up and shout, "Penne!," "Lasagna!," and "Welcome to *Name that Noodle!*, the game show that tests your knowledge of pasta!"

A critical skill to shelving your ego is listening. As a matter of fact, listening is the foundation of being able to think on your feet. Adapting in the moment requires that you really hear and understand what is going on. That's much easier said than done. Listening in the moment is an art in itself. Most American adults listen to only the first half of any sentence before they start thinking about their response, their opinion, lunch, or some other unrelated distraction.

We usually spend our brain time in memories of the past or plans for the future. That's why improvisation is such an important skill. It demands that you stay in the present.

We've all seen—or been—the person just dying to look smart. You're in the boardroom and the big cheese says something that creates a connection for you. You have a sharp response! You're going to finally look prepared, intelligent, or humorous, whenever you get the chance to add your two cents. You're focused on your comment and waiting impatiently for your chance to speak up. Unfortunately, you've also missed the next four things said around the table. Sometimes, really listening also means giving up your smart response, because by truly listening and shelving your ego, you're following the flow of ideas closely enough to understand that your comment may not be relevant or right in the moment.

One of the best examples of shelving your ego I ever saw in the workplace occurred at one of the largest health systems in the United States. One of the executives had an excellent staff of almost one hundred. Retention was close to 98 percent and the team was constantly winning internal awards for performance. We were there to focus on their good work and to look for ways to spread the model throughout the enterprise.

As I observed meetings of this group, I marveled at their improvisational and trusting behaviors. In particular, the head of the group often kicked off meetings with a "throw." She would chat with everyone for a while and then throw out a question, a goal, or an idea. Then she sat back. Her team was so accustomed to jumping in to play that she could relax and watch it happen. She shelved her ego so that others could lead and be heard.

One particular meeting was especially telling. The executive came in with a plan for the very important rollout of a handheld technology. It was practically baked, and it had her fingerprints all over it. At one point, a team member suggested an alternative to phase one that would require a complete makeover of the whole plan. The executive was definitely taken aback and didn't try to hide the uncertainty on her face. However, instead of putting on the brakes and saying, "We're under deadline. Let's just get this thing rolling," she let the team run with the new idea.

Believe me, she was nervous, and she tasked the team with proving that the alternative would create a faster, more efficient rollout. She gave them two days to rework it and bring back their findings. When the team came back excited, with all the reasons why they should change the plan, she did not hesitate for a second. And it was a very successful rollout.

This executive was an incredible example of a leader whose focus was on the good of the project rather than on her version of "right." She shelved her ego so that the team would feel free to mess with her work, knowing she'd assess it fairly and not feel hurt that it needed to be changed.

Some people might argue that the ego doesn't matter if the leader is effective. Yet, if an entire organization is about one ego, what happens when the ego goes away? Jim Collins, author of *Good to Great*, gives example after example of companies that achieved greatness and stayed great because their leaders shelved their egos. These understated leaders allowed others in their organization to shine, and the culture was about the team, not the leader. In these instances, companies continued to excel well after the tenure of the leader had passed, although the leaders' contributions were certainly remembered and credited. By contrast, Collins also reports on organizations that rose to greatness under a high-powered personality. Unfortunately, many of those organizations could not maintain their greatness after the leader left.[3]

Building Blocks can't happen unless you shelve your ego on a regular basis. Having the flexibility to play many roles is critical to innovation, great leadership, and trust. When a teams know that you will either lead, step back, or support based on the good of the project, they can trust, take risks, and create on a very high level.

Bring a Block

After you've jumped in to play, said the word *and*, and shelved your ego, guess what? You need to contribute something! This is where the skin in the game really happens. Your creative juice, your connected idea, and your responsibility for success all rely on the block that you bring. The good news is that bringing a block is really about contributing something every time you get a chance.

There will be times when we contribute a lot—we've prepared and planned, our colleagues know we have responsibility, and we've put a great deal of work into the block that we bring. There also will be times when our contribution is very small but nonetheless important. Perhaps you spoke up in a meeting or supported others in a way that is never publicly recognized. The point is to contribute. Bring something, even if it makes you nervous.

The best part of bringing a block is that it can be a tiny commitment at first. Just one block and you get to be part of the team. You get a place at the table. Very simple ideas build complex whole things, and it just takes one block at a time. Think about the fact that all of the things in the entire universe—the unbelievably complex, surprising universe—comprise only 115 elements. Of course, those 115 are simply all that have been proven at present; there are other elements that scientists are still looking for, considering, and disputing. Who knows when another Building Block will be found? That's the power of Building Blocks. Bring a block, and you never know where it will all go.

⁂ Ideas are like rabbits. You get a couple and learn how to handle them, and pretty soon you have a dozen.

JOHN STEINBECK

Suppose you try to engage in a Building Blocks session. Think about how that might feel. A colleague throws out an idea that you're really uncertain about, but you jump in and play, saying, "Yes, and . . ." You shelve your ego and then bring a block by adding the first thing that pops into your head that connects to the original idea.

It's tough at first. You want to take the conversation in a direction that's yours, toward what you think is best, but you relentlessly agree to stay in it with your colleague. Soon, the idea has grown, and it starts to feel like your idea too. You've added as many details as your colleague and you are both getting excited. This idea has real potential, real legs to it, and you've both got a stake in bringing it to this point. It all came from focus, from Building Blocks, from saying "Yes, and" and sticking with the exercise.

One of the best real-life examples of Building Blocks, without a doubt, is the Linux operating system. Linus Torvalds created the Linux kernel in 1991 and then made the code entirely public, so any software programmer can get in, see the details, and add his or her own piece. Believe me, anyone interested in this project was dying to jump in and play, and there were many times when programmers shelved their egos because another person had found a more elegant piece of code to replace theirs. Ultimately, hundreds of people brought a block. Linux became a wildly effective, efficient piece of programming because there was an unlimited amount of collaboration going on within a Building Blocks mentality.

When an organization has a strong mission, vision, or brand, that clarity can create a really powerful Building Blocks culture. We've had the privilege to work with a few such organizations. For example, one company that employs over one hundred thousand people globally maintains a singular focus on ethics and excellence. Its leaders constantly remind their people, train their people, and engage the opinions of their people, seeking to be the most ethical and excellent service provider in the market. They clearly define what that means on a day-to-day basis. As a result, whenever someone is considering a task or project, they can hold it up to the corporate identity: "Does the block I'm about to bring to the table support our drive to be the most ethical and excellent provider in our market? Does my new block dilute that message or make it stronger?" When employees understand the powerful idea that every small action connects to the big picture, they are able to pursue their company's vision with every block they bring in, every minute of their day.

✳ Towers Perrin conducted a study involving 10,333 employees of midsized to large companies in thirteen countries and found that, after opportunity and well-being, trust was the most critical indicator of employee engagement: "Trust, meaning that employees believed they worked for people with integrity, especially their direct supervisors. It was also important for employees to feel that people at their level in the organization were trusted and respected by management."

ADRIAN GOSTICK AND
CHESTER ELTON[4]

Bringing a block makes us part of the performance. This means we're now responsible for the success of the show and we'd better be engaged. If we zone out and let the performance tank, we're going to look really stupid in front of hundreds of audience members.

It's easy to get comfortable with staying on the sidelines, cheering on someone else doing the work, and going home without caring whether we won or lost. If you don't feel valued or involved, it's easy to disengage, collect a paycheck, and do as little as possible. I believe that we all would prefer to work with people—and to *be* people—who pick up the ball and run it downfield. The scary part is the risk. If you pick up the ball, you might get dirty. You might fumble. You might lose the game. Saying "and" not only involves risk; it also demands that you trust your team to support you. You believe that they'll stop any threats, share your goal, and pick you up and put you back in the game if you fail.

Get in there. Play. Contribute. All that, thanks to the little word *and*.

"Yes, but" Is Not "Yes, and"

Small things matter. And the Building Blocks concept demonstrates that every action, every block you bring, can have an effect. Therefore, the fact that "Yes, but" is not "Yes, and" is a very important point.

"Yes, but" is the ugly cousin of "Yes, and" and is an insidious killer of positivity. Have you ever shared a new thought with someone, watched them nodding and smiling, and thought they were really on board with you? The listener says, "Yes, I get it!" (a moment of elation for you) and then, "But it will never work."

Torpedo. You feel not only denied but also patronized.

"Yes! What a wonderful idea. But we don't have time right now."

"Yes! What a well-written proposal. But we have no budget for new projects."

"Yes! That's a great jacket. But do you really want to wear it to the office?"

Consider performance review time. You're getting all this great feedback. You're feeling valued. Your manager is saying, "Yes! We loved the work you did on the Acme account. You were so thorough, and the client loved you. But . . ."

It doesn't really matter what comes next. All you know is that what came first was bull. Your manager was trying to make the bad news easier on you and trying to find a more comfortable way to get through the conversation herself.

I'll take some fire for my opinion, but this is one of the worst feedback mechanisms I've ever encountered. Thousands of managers and human resources professionals are trained to give a "but sandwich" when providing feedback: Give them a compliment. Give them the bad news and your suggestion for improvement. Give them another compliment as they head out the door.

Yuck.

In real life, it sounds like this: "Wow, Nina, you've done some great work on the RedBlue project. I like the new format for measurements. But our line workers are used to the old format and don't want to change to a new way of reading their information, even though it saves time on your end. So we'll have to have you manually put everything back into the old format, OK? Thanks for the great work, and keep it up with the good ideas! One will stick one of these days!"

Monitor your "Yes, but" activity. When you become aware of it, the words will begin to stand out in high relief. Understand that every time that nasty word *but* shows up, somebody is being denied. Castles are being ripped down and you look like a know-it-all. And *but* assumes other disguises, such as the devil's advocate. For some reason, we've given anyone the right to kill progress and positivity by playing the devil's advocate. They always get to look smart and discerning, yet they're just serving us a big plate of denial.

Building Blocks demands that we focus on the idea now, stay in the moment, and see how far we can take it. We have a propensity to hear something and immediately decide what is wrong or how we will phrase our rebuttal. Try suspending that urge just once. Hear the suggestion. Nod and repeat it in your head. Then, instead of saying "But," "Well," or "I don't know," say "And."

"I thought we might try that new vegetarian restaurant." To which the steak lover responds, "Yes, *and* I'll even try some tofu."

"Will you play a game with me?" To which the adult absorbed in work e-mail on a Saturday will say, "Yes, *and* let's go pick it out together."

"I want to consider a vendor we've never used before." To which the manager responds, "Yes, *and* I'll help you with some due diligence on their capabilities."

If you have negative news, be open and honest. Let your colleagues know what the issue is and ask them to be part of the solution. Tough conversations are hard to get through, but honesty and straightforwardness show much more respect.

Focus and Building Blocks

We can accomplish so much more in business and life with a little more focus. A willingness to go with the idea of a trusted companion, support it, add our own creativity, and watch it play out may be one of the finest skills we can learn.

Focus is a dying art. As a population, we are losing the ability to stick with something and see it to its finish. We want high-level details and low time commitment. With the sheer volume of information available, we have exchanged depth for breadth.

It seems that we've managed to transform ourselves into what playwright Richard Foreman calls "'pancake people'—spread wide and thin as we connect with that vast network of information accessed by the mere touch of a button."[5] So we hop from one subject to the next, from one blog to another task to another conversation. We are slaves to the digital devices that become more important than the living, breathing people standing right in front of us.

This pressure to multitask and the contemporary demands on our attention are affecting us deeply. Often, we look at the thinnest, topmost layer of an idea and discard it. Or we become distracted with too many projects, priorities, and ideas.

The concept that multitaskers get more done is a myth. Multitaskers may get more *tasks* accomplished, but they are not generating better, more strategic, or more creative solutions to anything. We are losing our focus, and that is extending beyond our everyday tasks to our sense of self. We are not building castles for ourselves, our families, or our work.

Dr. Glenn Wilson, a psychiatrist at King's College London, conducted a fascinating study of the effects of multitasking on human IQ. In over eighty clinical trials with more than 1,100 people, Wilson found significant short-term loss of IQ during multitasking. As a matter of fact, the ability to think, reason, and do good work was worse in multitaskers than in a group of marijuana smokers. The average IQ loss among multitaskers was measured at ten points—more than double the average four-point loss found among cannabis users.[6] Late-night talk show hosts would have a carnival with that one.

What this really means is that our lack of focus is actually deteriorating our ability to think and work. Between the ringing phone, the beeping text, the incoming e-mail, and the shuttling of family to the doctor or the soccer field in between conference calls we mute so that we can write proposals and make dinner and respond to the people popping into our office or home, we're losing our intelligence. Temporarily.

We're also losing the trust of the people around us. If we can't focus and get the job done, people begin to doubt our abilities. They wonder if they can rely on us.

I worked with a young associate at a global professional services firm who aptly demonstrated just how much multitasking can affect trust in a relationship. This woman reported to two different partners in the firm. She described what it was like to go into their offices to speak with each of them.

"When I go in to talk to Jason, he always gives me his attention. He's an incredibly important person at the firm, but whenever I'm in his office he puts down the cover of his laptop, mutes the ringer on his phone, leans forward, and makes eye contact. I can't tell you how good it makes me feel, and how much I want to do great work for him!

"But when I go in to talk to April, she never stops doing all the activities she's engaged in. She keeps her eyes on her computer, continuing to type e-mail, and interrupts our conversation any time the phone rings or she gets a text. If I'm listing important information, I ask her if I need to write it down for her. She refuses and says, 'I've got it, I've got it. Keep going.' But she doesn't have it!"

She recounted how many times April had missed details, forcing her to scramble to keep a project together. It was nerve wracking and she worried that it would reflect badly on her rather than on her manager.

She told me she felt as though she were two people at work. It's difficult enough to report to two people, but she also found that she acted differently, depending on which boss she was working for at any given moment. Just knowing that she had to talk to April made her feel anxious. She consistently did redundant work and worked more hours on April's projects, and she felt a good deal of stress. On the other hand, although her projects for Jason also were demanding and stressful, she always had a sense of underlying confidence that the job would get done and that she could rely on his leadership.

The firm has two excellent partners in April and Jason. However, their everyday behaviors are affecting the bottom line. Because of their worry about April being spread thin, her associates are billing more hours than they should and are doing redundant work.

Focus. We need it, and Building Blocks provides a format to achieve it while also collaborating. Jump in and play, shelve your ego, and bring a block.

Building Blocks in Real Life

It's not easy to engage in "Yes, and." It's uncomfortable, challenging, and sometimes scary. If we don't try it, however, we'll never learn how to break out of our old, negative patterns of behavior.

You may be thinking, "Building Blocks seems like a good idea, and it's clear that 'Yes, and' works onstage. But what about in real life? What does 'Yes, and' look like there?" Let's consider the story of someone with a very nonstandard workplace.

Barb Lauer does really intense work. Her office is sometimes a war zone and her clients may not have enough to eat or a place to sleep. Some of us work for corporations; Barb works for nongovernmental organizations. Such groups may be for-profit or nonprofit, but all try to create improvement and change during crisis.

Despite her unusual work environment, Lauer has used "Yes, and" as a transformational tool throughout her career in Afghanistan, the Balkans, Indonesia, Liberia, and Russia. She currently is a social worker for Development Alternatives Inc. and goes to communities in crisis, often in war. She learned about the improviser's mind-set from an improviser friend of mine, Eric Berg, in the late 1980s, and she went on to apply the concepts to her work. She has supported organizational and social change using the three Building Blocks: jump in and play, shelve your ego, and bring a block.

Lauer told me, "There are so many cross-cultural barriers we face as social workers in another country. Terrible gender and power barriers. Someone says something that creates defensiveness or makes the speaker appear to be acting superior, and everything stops. When I am trying to build a relationship, I say, 'Yes, that's a good point. And we could integrate your idea into our solution this way. What do you think?'"

During such conversations, Lauer says, she can see that her acknowledgement of the other person allows him or her to become relevant. It levels the power and the gender dynamic, and then Lauer becomes relevant, too. In countries with the most extreme oppression, she's seen people's faces light up, just because of "Yes, and."

Now, if Lauer can create a relationship that bridges cultures, genders, and crises by using "Yes, and," how can it be too hard for us? We've all been in conversations like the one she describes. Someone gets offended or put off and every-thing stops—the conversation, the negotiation, and the rela-tionship. If we apply the Building Blocks concept, we can get the results Lauer has seen for years.

Lauer worked in Liberia in 2006 and 2007, assisting the new cabinet of President Ellen Johnson Sirleaf. A couple of seventeen-year-old boys came to her and said they wanted to form a student parliament. Their goal was to look at issues affecting youth and then to bring their ideas and opinions to the real, elected parliament. They wanted to form a strong lobbying force for youth.

Lauer's gut reaction was negative. Her mind was imme-diately overwhelmed with concerns. For example, she knew that although President Sirleaf was working to change the tone of government in Liberia, the previous administrations had been more politicians than advocates of the people. She also knew that promises made by politicians often were not kept. She did not want these youths to be disappointed.

She also was taken aback by the scope of their dream. They wanted youths from every area to attend, and they wanted to get the process off the ground in a big way, imme-diately. Lauer knew from experience how difficult the logis-tics of even a simple meeting could be in Liberia. Planning, communication, and transportation all were very slow and difficult to coordinate. She feared that if she let them try, the initiative would fail and that such a failure would dam-age their belief in, involvement with, and support of their government.

Instead, she took a deep breath, and said, "Yes, and tell me more about why you are interested." The boys had excellent reasons. She said "Yes, and" again and asked another question. They thought and brainstormed, and again they had an excellent response. As much as Lauer hoped that the students would slow down and take a smaller project, a baby step first, they were committed to flying.

During the following months, the students worked on making their parliament a reality. Every time a barrier arose, Lauer just handed it back to them: "Yes, and tell me how you think we can get other youths engaged in this?" And the teenagers came up with all of the answers.

The first student parliament of Liberia comprised one hundred teens from Guinea, Liberia, and Sierra Leone. This was an unexpected success. The students discussed issues that affected them directly, such as the use of child soldiers and their desire to attend school longer.

It went so well that they did it again. The second parliament occurred only in Liberia, and this was a particular triumph. The teens invited six adult members of their government parliament to attend. Although most of the adults who had been involved in coordinating the effort expected none of the politicians to show up, all six participated. The parliament members were asked questions they'd never heard before, and although the teens remained respectful, it was a strong, breakthrough experience for everyone.

Lauer recalls, "I could feel the kids begin to understand, start to see and realize what politics, government, civic responsibility could mean to them. To their futures. They understood that they could have a voice. I take no credit—not one whit—for this. All of the ideas were theirs. I just kept saying 'Yes, and.'"

What Lauer fails to take credit for is that if she hadn't said "Yes, and" that very first day, the student parliament might never have occurred.

Lauer shared a final key thought with me: "There is so much wisdom in other people. They have all the answers they need. I just have to help them find it. It's really my job to say 'Yes, and.' It actually seems a bit arrogant to say anything other than 'Yes, and.' I have to turn off the arrogance and maximize the moment. We should all be using 'Yes, and,' trusting in the wisdom of the people around us. I've only done what we should all do every day."

When Lauer has used "Yes, and," she's made people who've lived their entire lives in oppression feel relevant. She's opened a door for them to trust her, and for her to trust them. She's helped people rebuild homes and lives after terrible devastation. Now, obviously that's not all because of "Yes, and." There also are Lauer's years of hard work, education, experience, and negotiation. Still, she's lived her life as an improviser—with stakes far higher than just a good performance.

Building Blocks Case Study: Legg Mason

Everything was changing for Legg Mason, a regional, family-oriented brokerage firm in Baltimore. A historic swap with Citigroup in 2005 made it a much more complicated firm. Legg Mason bought Citi's asset management practice and swapped out its broker/dealer business to Citigroup. In that move, the new Legg Mason Asset Management became a pure-play asset management firm. It worked strictly as a wholesaler to financial advisors and individuals across the world who created funds and investments for themselves and their clients.

It was an excellent business choice, but the acquisition/merger represented an enormous cultural challenge. Legg Mason employees were used to a small, regional atmosphere, whereas the Citigroup employees came from a 330,000-person global enterprise. In addition, the new Legg Mason Asset Management had to market to tens of thousands of new potential clients—financial advisors and investors who had never heard of them. Employees of the new firm were confused about how to represent themselves—for whom did they really work?

Adding to the difficulty was Legg Mason's unusual structure. Over time, it had become a firm of firms, offering many different investment choices. Under its umbrella were firms such as Brandywine, Clearbridge, Permal, and Royce. However, unlike many other parent companies that acquire smaller groups and force them to change, Legg Mason allowed its affiliates to retain their names, structures, and autonomy, to support their continued success.

It was complicated. And guess what—complexity is hard to sell. Especially if you have two minutes to convince a very busy financial advisor that he or she should hear about the financial products you have to offer but you can't get past a rambling story about the merger, the other firms, the new name, and so on. Salespeople were being met with a confused frown and "Now, where did you say you're from?"

That's a moment of truth for a salesperson. One of the critical tools in any salesperson's kit is the elevator pitch.

That term, elevator pitch, comes from the idea of unexpected opportunity. If you accidentally end up on an elevator with a key client, you must be able to clearly identify who you are, what you do, and why they should care, in the space of a few floors. That first Building Block of sales success was missing for Legg Mason.

Jump in and Play at Legg Mason

The marketing team at Legg Mason responded; however, they didn't want to go about this initiative in the same old way. They wanted to engage their employees and create a compelling story for the marketplace, and they had to do it in a way that would be both memorable and effective. Legg Mason hired Ologie, a marketing strategist, to create a new brand for Legg Mason.

For this effort to be a success, people had to believe in and adopt the new story. And because, ultimately, this initiative was about storytelling, Bill Faust, partner and chief strategy officer at Ologie, says, "This wasn't a situation where you could read about or listen to a presentation and deliver. In order to learn how to tell a story, you have to do it—out loud and in front of other people. Not to mention that you never know how the listener will react."

ImprovEdge was the next block in the initiative. We worked with the combined teams to create a workshop that not only would inform participants about the critical importance of a clear brand but also would enable them to learn and practice their new story.

The story came in three successive blocks—a thirty-second introduction, a five-minute story, and a twenty-minute presentation. Each was a version of the other and told the Legg Mason Asset Management story consistently, but with different levels of detail. Managing Director Benji Baer, who led the effort for Legg Mason, says, "The most important thing we needed to accomplish was to give our wholesalers a greater sense of confidence in the field. Salespeople always need a new reason to reach out to potential clients, and the brand confusion was creating a barrier to effective communication. By cleaning up the brand and story, we removed that barrier and gave them the confidence to get out there and tell a compelling story. Our people had to come out with the three Cs: confidence, conviction, and consistency."

I worked with a skeptical leader, Kathleen Pritchard, during our first meetings to prepare the program. I watched her frown and consider for a few moments, then shrug and take a leap. She jumped in to play and began improvising with us, and she quickly became one of our greatest advocates. With astonishing speed she moved from jumping in, to shelving her ego, to contributing her ideas about shaping the workshop for best results. The entire Legg Mason prep team jumped in fully and was highly committed to excellence. We ran more pilot programs than we ever have, and the workshop was eventually rolled out to over 1,300 sales employees.

We knew that the first thing we would have to do was play. We had to break the ice with these financially minded participants and get them up on their feet. The experience started out as informative and progressively became more kinetic. By introducing play, we brought everyone along with us. All the old cultures fell away and participants played side by side, sharing laughter and ideas and starting to form their own, new culture.

One of the games we used is called Sign Pass. Participants must choose a nonverbal sign that represents who they are; during the game, they show their own sign, mimic someone else's sign, or throw the sign to someone else. If you ever played Thumper in college, it's a close cousin to that game. Sign Pass is a warm-up game that not only enables adults to enter a safe place to play but also helps them reveal aspects of themselves they don't normally share. It seems like a small thing, but after participants learn that a colleague loves to cook or work on motorcycles, they form a strong new point of connection. Those little bits of knowledge enable them to feel more known and to create new, trusting bonds with their colleagues. At Legg Mason, Sign Pass was the first block in creating a cohesive new culture.

Shelve Your Ego at Legg Mason

Believe it or not, the very first group to go through the finalized Legg Mason workshop was the executive team. To have the most senior leaders of a large enterprise shelve their egos and go through a game-based workshop is an impressive show of commitment. They did not say, "Oh, this is just for the field wholesalers and I'm too busy." Instead, they believed that they needed to understand the story too, and to be as vulnerable as their employees. The unexpected outcome of this participation was that the leadership team became spokespeople for the initiative. They could speak firsthand about the experience and they got their field leaders excited about it. In fact, they insisted that the experience extend beyond the wholesalers to the entire company—then everyone could be a mouthpiece for the organization.

As the workshops rolled out nationwide, we found that it was difficult for some people to let go of their old identity. The Citigroup name is instantly recognized, and for salespeople trying to grab attention, it was sometimes easier to tell the story of an individual firm. Becoming part of the new Legg Mason Asset Management meant giving up an old story that might have worked and felt comfortable. Everybody had to put the past behind them at some point and commit to a new identity.

As facilitators of these change workshops, we were consistently impressed with the level of engagement we saw in all the participants. They admitted that this was hard, but everyone was determined to become a great firm.

One of the sales leaders from the field participated in the very first workshop. A week later, he came back with an incredible success story. A day after the workshop, he found himself at a backyard barbecue chatting with a neighbor, who asked the inevitable "Now, what do you do again?" The leader was tempted to say, "I'm in finance" and leave it at that, but he had just been through this workshop about using his new story! He took a deep breath and used the first block—his new elevator pitch.

The neighbor seemed interested and asked a question. The salesman went into more detail, in a very relaxed, friendly kind of way. The conversation continued and then eventually moved to other topics. Yet, later that week, the salesman learned that his neighbor had called up his own financial advisor and had bought Legg Mason funds. Because the salesman took the risk and shelved his ego to use a new, effective elevator pitch, a sale had been made.

The workshop also included some risky elements, by design. Through exercises and role playing, participants were placed in very difficult situations in which they had to practice their new skills at telling the Legg Mason story. We pushed them into conflicted and confusing situations based on real incidents from the field and did not make it easy on them—far better to fall down and try again in the safety of the workshop than to stumble out in the field. Mark Fetting, a senior executive vice president at the time, remembers, "The use of improvisation was a superb technique. We were all made vulnerable and had to start at square one together. All of us in the field felt bonded by it, and we felt closer to our counterparts in the offices. It was fantastic!"

Near the end of the workshop rollout, Fetting was chosen as chairman and chief executive officer of Legg Mason, and every time I've observed and worked with him, he has embodied a Building Blocks mentality. He jumps in to play by engaging with his colleagues, he shelves his ego by always listening to both his employees and the market, and he consistently brings his best to the table. In a moment of wry commentary, he summed up the importance of the Legg Mason story elevator pitch: "If you can't make the intro, you ain't getting the deal."

Bringing a Block at Legg Mason

Legg Mason has a powerful story to tell, but it only works if each person tells the story consistently. Every time someone starts to talk about Legg Mason, it's a moment of possibility, a chance to create clarity and presence. And it all relies on the people.

As Pritchard notes, "We *are* the building blocks of Legg Mason. We don't offer products that you can hold, touch, or on which you can push buttons. We offer an intangible but powerful service. People are the living embodiment of the brand. We have to be able to represent who we are just as powerfully as any brand does with a logo."

I have been pleased to hear about the outcomes of Legg Mason's improvisational plunge. The metrics after the workshops included tracking many more new clients—the rapid growth of financial advisors investing in Legg Mason funds. Sales productivity in the field also increased. However, it was a few surprise metrics that I most enjoyed learning about. Fetting notes that those who went through the exercises exhibited a better spirit of humor and engagement and seemed to have greater trust in the organization. Fetting also says, "This initiative was one of the building blocks of my own career. The success we enjoyed in the field was one of the reasons I was chosen to lead Legg Mason as CEO."

You never know where Building Blocks will go, but you can be sure that they will build something. Sometimes it's the foundation for a structure you never expected.

Building Blocks Behaviors

The following behaviors and exercise are simple ways to put Building Blocks into practice. Try them out, take it slowly, and know that you can bring Building Blocks—that powerful *and*—into life. Dorothy Day once said, "People say, 'What is the sense of our small efforts?' They cannot see we must lay one brick at a time."

* Jump in and play.
  Say "Yes, and," then add your own piece or ask a question.

* Shelve your ego.
  Go along with someone else's idea today. Also, monitor "Yes, but" and be aware of how frequently you use this phrase.

* Bring a block.
  Ask what you can do in a situation where you usually don't have a role. Do some small thing for a colleague who's overwhelmed, such as copying a document or finishing a spreadsheet.

Building Blocks Exercise

Building Blocks Brainstorm[7]

Everybody needs to brainstorm sometimes. Maybe you need to come up with a name for a new project or service, or maybe you need to find ten creative new ways to entice people to visit your booth at a trade show. However, a Building Blocks session is not the same as a brainstorming session. In good brainstorming, you call out everything, anything, all the ideas you can muster. If you imagine every idea as a brick, a brainstorming session creates a big field full of bricks.

Instead, try tailoring the content to a single idea. You and your team want to see just how far one idea can be pushed and to create a complete reality based on the first suggestion. If every contribution in a Building Blocks session is a brick, you'll end up with a castle. Try this exercise the next time you need to brainstorm.

Get Ready

1. Some of the rules of brainstorming apply here; for instance, there are no edits and everybody plays. The

difference is that everyone will focus on the initial idea.

2. Clearly state the idea that you're going to build. You might determine, for example, "We want to make our boring product, the toilet brush, more interesting."

Get Set

3. Enable everyone to contribute by going around the group. Keep it flexible enough that someone can pass if he or she is stuck and that someone with an immediate contribution can speak up.

4. Start with a single contribution, such as "Let's give our toilet brush a name and personality."

Go

5. Let the ideas roll. "Let's get our brush, Trixie, a page on Facebook. And let's post funny pictures of her on vacation or doing her job—cleaning a toilet. Let's have her connected to other named versions of our products on social networking sites."

6. If you are the facilitator, keep the energy high by encouraging each contribution and pulling in everyone. Let your wild ideas go far, and keep adding. Remember, one person's impossibility is another person's invention.

Chapter Three

The Third Secret of Improvisation

Team Equity

She exclaims, "Yes! And I'll have the photo-synthesis shake with a side of good topsoil."

The waiter writes on a pantomimed pad and then turns to you. You consider your menu before saying, "Well, gee, how about a nice salad?"

Everyone onstage looks at one another in shock. They follow the body language of the waiter, simultaneously letting out an audible gasp. All of them eye you, even the "furniture." The waiter is stepping back, clutching his heart.

"You are not . . . you are not a—"

"Vegetable cannibal!" your date, the Boston lettuce, shouts!

Without any consultation, your "chair" runs over to a piano in the corner, your date's "chair" grabs a microphone, and the two people forming the table start to dance in sync. The waiter pushes you against the wall, where you act as if you've been caught in a police sting. He starts to pantomime filming the whole thing.

The troupe member with the microphone follows the pianist's cue and starts to sing an improvised blues lament about the horrors of cannibalism. Your last troupe member, who has not been involved up to this point, comes to the front of the stage and translates the whole song into sign language.

What just happened? The third secret of improvisation: Team Equity.

The best part about working with an improv troupe is that it is just that—a troupe. A team. A group of people collaborating for a unified outcome. Someone always has your back, and there's always another set of brains on the job. It's the opposite of stand-up comedy, where one performer is alone with her material in front of an audience. Working in a team requires a critical set of skills to make it all work.

There are three elements of Team Equity:

* Own it

* Equity, not equality

* Tell it like it is

Own It

For a team to be really effective, everyone on the team has got to own it. And this means two things: the entire team must own both the people and the outcome. It's important to balance both. Focusing on just people or just outcome doesn't leverage the power of the team. A focus only on people means that the group isn't creating or producing, whereas a focus only on the outcome means that people don't offer their strengths or care about the team or product.

In my early days in network engineering sales, I worked for a manager who was very social. She knew everyone and their children, was kind and supportive, always organized events for us to enjoy, and was a pleasure to spend time with. Everyone on her team was loyal to her and loved working for her. Unfortunately, she lacked many of the capabilities needed to hit her targets, and quite honestly, she didn't seem to take outcomes very seriously. About six months into my new job I felt uneasy. I was very aware of the outcomes we needed to produce and was worried that my manager kept giving hall passes to team members who weren't hitting their numbers. It came as no surprise when eventually she was replaced.

On the other hand, I'm sure many of us have been in organizations that focus only on results—stock price, profit, sales. When everything is secondary to the outcome, people suffer, ethics are ignored, and teams develop tunnel vision. Sadly, the manager I've just described was replaced with her complete opposite: a manager who was aggressive, foul mouthed, and talked only about money. Believe me, we all hit our targets, but over the next twelve months I watched every member of the team leave for other positions, and I finally left as well. There's only so much abuse one can take.

So what's the balance?

In relation to the people in your group, owning it is about belonging and supporting. If you are part of a group but are not invested in working with, caring for, and developing the people in the group, you are only realizing a fraction of the group's power. High-performance teams know one another, learn about each member's talents and preferences, stand up for one another, and take responsibility for the actions of the team.

This was true in the vegetable scene: Owning it involved everybody. Every ensemble member was fully committed. From the moment the troupe arrived onstage, there never was a question of someone bailing out and leaving or standing there and doing nothing. The troupe members also knew they needed one another to make the show a success. No one person onstage could have created such an enjoyable scene alone. And even more interesting is that the ensemble did not know the outcome when the show started. They simply committed to doing it with all the passion and investment they had.

Groups of people who combine and then elevate their talents into a better whole are real teams. They are experts in their field, they enthusiastically practice and engage in their work, they take risks together, they all own it. And one of the strongest outcomes of those behaviors is trust. These teams accomplish so much because they trust that everyone on the team is owning it.

⋇ A team is a small number of people with complementary skills who are committed to a common purpose, performance goals, and approach for which they hold themselves mutually accountable.

JON R. KATZENBACH AND
DOUGLAS K. SMITH[1]

That cohesiveness also comes from everyone agreeing what "it" is. Teams need to regularly sit down and agree on the real goals for their jobs, their projects, and their company. Is "it" greater revenue? Or is "it" a new policy, a new initiative?

I once worked with a manager at a worldwide retailer who grumbled about a team member who "wasn't invested." This employee finished up her tasks and went home on time every day, even if others were staying late. The manager was angry because the goal—the "it" for him—was the completion of a special project, and the deadline was looming.

However, when I questioned the team member, she proudly told me that she was adhering to the company cost-cutting initiative. She previously had worked a lot of overtime but now was organized and focused and left promptly each day. Her "it" and the manager's "it" weren't aligned, so the team couldn't possibly perform well.

I brought them together and shared what I had learned from each individually. I was particularly impressed with the manager's response. He immediately thanked his team member for her efforts to keep expenses down and admitted he was sorry he hadn't asked questions sooner. Within a few minutes, they were crunching numbers and brainstorming. They quickly figured out that with only a few weeks of overtime for the team member, the entire project could be completed and much of the pressure taken off the other members of the team. By bringing in the project on time, the company ultimately would make far more money than it would save through a little less overtime. With that cohesive, global vision in mind, these two people and their team worked together better. They even brought the project in ahead of schedule!

Bringing the project in ahead of schedule certainly was a successful outcome. More importantly, however, by collaborating, being honest, and sharing needs, these team members also built a stronger relationship and created a trusting way to communicate. That relationship will continue to serve them throughout their careers together. It will enable them to perform at a high level again and again.

What about the results aspect of owning it? Outcome is the part of owning it that becomes the default objective for too many companies. The outcome becomes the only focus, to the detriment of process and relationships, which can make for a rotten workplace. Trust, commitment, and discretionary effort all deteriorate.

In its best sense, outcome is the result of great teamwork, collaboration, and improvisation. Every member of a great team understands his or her connection to the outcome. All team members understand that their part in it, no matter how small, is critical.

Jim Belasco wrote about the famous surgeon Denton Cooley. One day, when the author was shadowing the doctor on his rounds at the hospital, he observed Cooley stopping to talk to a janitor in the hallway. The surgeon and the man mopping the floor chatted for more than ten minutes. Finally, Cooley realized he was late and rushed off to the surgery suite. Belasco was curious and approached the janitor to talk.

"That was a long conversation," he said.

The man replied, "Dr. Cooley talks to me often."

The author inquired, "So, what do you do at the hospital?"

The janitor replied, "We save lives."[2]

Whenever I tell this story to a group, I pause after I quote the man mopping the hallway: "We save lives." Then I ask the group, "What did you think he was going to say?" Responses include "I'm the janitor" or "I mop the floors." No one expects this person to be so connected to the mission, the outcome of the hospital.

What an amazing person for this hospital to have on its team! He understands that by keeping the hospital mopped and clean every day he enables doctors and nurses to do their jobs. He has owned it—he feels connected to and responsible for his place of work, which is dedicated to saving lives. And in turn, Cooley, the pioneer of the artificial heart transplant, owned it when it came to knowing his team. He connected not only with his surgical colleagues but also with the cleaning staff and probably the nursing, administrative, cafeteria, and parking staff. The janitor and the doctor both were dedicated to building an equitable community.

Equity, Not Equality

Team Equity is about having all the right people in the right places, doing the right things. It is not about everybody having equal time, equal say in the matter, or equal skills. Members of high-performing teams complement each another. They are highly diverse in background, skills, and strength. They know their own strengths, the strengths of their team members, and how to leverage everyone's strength according to the situation.

The performance world gives us so many great examples of Team Equity at work. Constantin Stanislavski, cofounder of the Moscow Art Theatre, said, "There are no small parts, only small actors." What he meant was that a small part can be as wonderful and important as a big part, if you come to it with commitment and creativity. For example, Judi Dench won an Oscar for her eight-minute role in *Shakespeare in Love.*

When I studied Shakespeare at Oxford University, my dialect coach told me a story about going to see a stage production of *One Flew Over the Cuckoo's Nest,* a play set in an insane asylum. He told us about an incredible actor who was onstage throughout the entire production. He had no lines, no specific movement, and no interaction with any other actor onstage. He sat in the corner as one of the inmates of the asylum, mumbled to himself occasionally, and drooled. During the entire production, he never broke character, and more importantly, he never tried to be noticed or to be more than his character was supposed to be. He knew that, to do the best job he could and help make the play a success, his role was simply to be part of the asylum environment.

If that actor had tried to be noticed by the audience or had made himself louder than he should be, he would have spoiled the focus of the play. In the theater world, that's called upstaging. People would have been distracted by him and perhaps missed important things going on in the play. If you've ever watched a performance where you kept looking at the wrong person (a person who was not the focus of the story at the moment), they were upstaging the rest of the cast. Even the lead actor has to be still and quiet at times so that important moments have focus.

On the other side of this coin is the example of the small actor. Musicals.net has an entertaining discussion thread on Stanislavsky's quote. A person named Rachel posted this funny example of the epitome of a small actor: "I was in a play with a girl who spent every day complaining that she only had nine lines. She spent so much time complaining, that she never learned them. Literally. The day of the performance, I had to spend half an hour with her at rehearsal trying to get her to be able to remember them. We finally had to cut out half of them, so she was left with *four* lines."

This actor had every opportunity to be part of a great show, to do her best with the nine lines onstage, and to support the cast backstage during the rest of the show. Instead, she tried to make herself seem too important for a mere nine-line part. The outcome of her ridiculous behavior was that she became an actor no one would want to work with again.

In our improvisational workshops, we use a great exercise called the Two-Headed Expert. Two people link arms and must answer questions from their group. However, they can only say one word at a time, so the flow of words alternates between the two people, like this:

Person A: "I"

Person B: "am"

Person A: "the"

Person B: "two-"

Person A: "headed"

Person B: "expert!"

One person never knows what the other is going to say, but both must be committed to saying a grammatically correct sentence and answering questions supplied by the audience. The key here is that the answers do not have to be technically correct. If the topic was astrophysics and someone asked, "What is the foundational principle of astrophysics?," the two-headed expert could say, "The—foundational—principle—of—astrophysics—is—blueberry—pie." As long as they answer the question, and it is grammatically correct, they've played the game correctly.

One of the most interesting lessons of this game is the importance of each word. In the example above, the little word am is just as important as the bigger word expert. The sentence wouldn't work without either word, and it doesn't matter who says "am" and who says "expert." The point is to collaborate and build a working sentence.

It's funny and challenging, and the most successful duos let go of their assumptions, give up any control, and just say the next word that makes sense. When they relax and go with it, excellent answers flow right out. I've seen corporate employees who have never played a stage game in their life execute this game seamlessly and brilliantly, their colleagues howling with laughter at their off-the-cuff answers.

Improvisers call this being a passenger on the sentence. Both people realize that neither is the "conductor" driving the meaning or outcome. They are passengers on a train (the sentence) that will eventually arrive at the station (a completed answer). When they don't worry about control or "rightness," they can endlessly create working sentences simply by saying the next best word. They literally give themselves over to total collaboration.

A big part of that collaboration involves real listening: listening without judgment or pause. Many individuals stumble in this game because they just can't believe what they've heard. They get stuck on the answer they hear in their head rather than listening and going with their partner's contribution. They try to throw in two words to force the sentence to go their way, or they pause in consternation, unable to loosen their brains enough to go along with the unexpected word.

If the game falls apart, it's usually because one of the heads is trying to gain control. They say silly words out of context in order to be noticed or to throw off the game. They don't want to say "to"; they want to say "hippopotamus"! In trying too hard to look funny, they actually look stupid and ruin the game.

Or sometimes a participant is reluctant to let go because

he or she really is an expert. I once used this exercise with a large steel manufacturer. The audience called out golf as the topic, and one of the volunteers just happened to play a lot of golf. It seemed almost impossible for him to give up control. I watched as he elbowed his partner and whispered answers to him. He was so concerned about a correct answer that he almost couldn't play the game.

When it was over, we talked about his frustration. I asked a lot of questions and eventually this man realized that the game wasn't about being right; it was about collaborating. He had a big "Aha!" moment and asked to play again. He did far better the second time, and we also let him practice with a topic he knew nothing about. After he had viscerally experienced what it was like to give up control and still succeed, he had another "Aha!" moment. After the workshop, he told me that at work he focused on never making a mistake rather than on creating a great project. His new commitment to himself was to try to be a passenger on his team's projects rather than squelching activity out of the fear that it would be wrong.

This ability to do whatever it takes for the good of the whole is one of the most unsung attributes of high-performance teams. In the vegetable scene, playing the part of a piece of furniture is not exactly a great moment in the spotlight. However, the troupe members didn't care because they were committed to the overall performance. In addition, each had a chance to take on a more interesting role later because they played their first part very well. They realized that they could pull off a great performance if everybody rose to the occasion. The ensemble also used its very diverse talents and capabilities: one could sing, one could play piano, a few could dance. They didn't try to take on a role in which they'd fail—they leveraged individual qualities to create an excellent whole.

✳ There are precious few Einsteins among us. Most brilliance arises from ordinary people working together in extraordinary ways.

ROGER VON OECH[3]

This understanding is realized exceptionally well in the internship program of one of our clients, a national retailer. Interns are not given very glamorous work, nor are they paid terribly well. However, the company does an extraordinary job of informing the interns about the effect of their work. They are taken on long tours so that they can see exactly what happens to their spreadsheet, their memo, or their product specification. They follow the chain right to a satisfied customer. In addition, the interns are rewarded for completing the most thankless work in an exceptional way, especially when it's a team effort. An intern once looked at me and said, "I never thought anyone could have fun and feel motivated stuffing envelopes. I think I've learned more this summer than in all of my other internships combined!"

When we think of work teams that perform well, these

words come to mind: *excellence, performance, competence,* and *investment.* Another secret most people don't know about improv is that good improvisers are often the most over-rehearsed people in the industry. Talk about an investment in preparation and time. They never know what will happen onstage, so they constantly practice, play, rehearse, and risk to be ready for anything.

And remember, equity is not equality. We worked specifically on Team Equity within a large financial organization. The sales team had a culture that supported giving everyone a chance to do everything and using resources based on regional proximity. Unfortunately, their outcomes were showing that a culture of equality in the field was not serving them well. For example, a big client pitch for mortgages came up in the mid-Atlantic region. John had never pitched a client, but he lived right there and so he presented at the meeting. That's fair, right? Unfortunately, the client got a terrible presentation from a novice and the company lost the business. John just didn't have the skills and experience to close the deal.

By using the concept of equity not equality, the company was able to change its culture for better outcomes. The team identified its specific strengths and skills so that everyone nationwide knew who to turn to for the best strength in each area, such as presentation skills or mortgage deals. In every situation, a project or pitch was assessed and a team assembled that would offer the greatest strength and the complementary talents to get the deal done.

As a result, people began to feel more fulfilled and

excited. If a person's passion and strength was internal work, they previously had found it terribly uncomfortable to pitch to clients and devastating to lose a deal. Now the team could support the right people in a way that leveraged its strengths.

Team Equity at work.

Tell It Like It Is

Feedback is a gift. Although it can seem hard to hear at times, if feedback is given with positive intent and is meant to help you improve, it is a gift. You can consider it, keep it, amend it, use it, or toss it away, but no matter what, it will give you a little more insight into yourself.

Telling it like it is means immediate honesty with your team, provided with the intention of getting better. Believe it or not, it's easier to receive feedback than to give it. Giving feedback is uncomfortable, it's hard to do right, and most people prefer to avoid difficult conversations.

Telling it like it is in improv is very immediate and is actually far easier to understand because our work is in front of everyone and we know how it's going from moment to moment. The first feedback we get is onstage, in the reaction of the audience. They are either laughing or they're not. They are either leaning forward, watching the stage, or they're checking their phones for texts.

Telling it like it is is also about "taking a note." Debriefing and notes are an intrinsic part of the performance community. After every performance, the leader or director of the troupe is responsible for giving notes. Every performance is debriefed that night, or no more than twenty-four hours later, so that the performance and any issues are fresh in everyone's mind and adjustments can be made quickly.

I once was part of a great, short-lived improv troupe in Chicago called Tribe. Our director sat in the audience, and even though some of our performances didn't finish until midnight, we all stayed late for notes. We were immediately, intensely concerned with getting feedback so the next night would be better.

Being open to taking those notes isn't easy. Almost every performer can relay a story about an individual who couldn't drop his or her ego to take the note. The point in development and notes is to listen, adjust, change, and get better. Then move on. I've been in many debriefing sessions in the wee hours of the morning, exhausted after a show, when someone was dragging it out, arguing or not accepting feedback. That's usually the point when the entire ensemble chimes in, "Take the note!"

The Blue Angels, a U.S. Navy flight demonstration squadron, have a ritual of the "nameless, rankless debrief" after every show. Since 1946, they have assisted in the recruiting and goodwill efforts of the navy and the armed forces, in front of millions of viewers. These teams of pilots fly in perfect, breathtaking formation for shows throughout the year. Their maneuvers are unimaginable—they swoop, dive, and fly mere inches from each other, in perfect formation, at unbelievable speeds. The debriefing, in which pilots literally remove their stripes, often goes on for hours after a show. They discuss every detail of the flight and decide how to improve, stay sharp, and manage the danger of the job.

Incidentally, theater directors are not always popular people. A big part of their job, of getting the best ensemble and the best performance possible, is telling it like it is. Nonetheless, most actors I know actually prefer a more straightforward approach.

I worked on a production where we unexpectedly had to switch directors in the middle of the rehearsal process, and it was a good thing we did! Our original director was a great guy, artistically experienced and fun to work with. However, he only made suggestions, never stepped on toes, and ultimately left character decisions up to the actors. The new director had a clear vision for the show and the characters, told us exactly what she wanted, and didn't mince words when it came to things that didn't work. It was a shock, but the show came together much more quickly and got excellent reviews. It's important to note that she was also experienced and fun to work with. She wasn't a tyrant by any means, but she brought her strength to the table without reservation. And that strength was telling it like it is.

The immediacy of feedback seems to have been lost in many work environments. Projects only receive "postmortem" reviews. That's when it's too late, as the awful term *postmortem* indicates. Worse yet, I've seen environments where only problems or failures are debriefed. One of the key elements of review is focusing on strengths and positive outcomes so that they can be replicated. Telling it like it is must be applied to both the positive and the negative.

In the work environment, there should never be surprises at review time. People deserve to know how they are doing every day. This is difficult for a lot of managers, because people don't like delivering tough news. A performance issue often is discussed with the individual's manager and human resources representative but not with the individual! That person is the proverbial last one to know.

Even if it is something as simple as bad grammar in a proposal or coming to work late, people don't want to talk to their colleagues about weaknesses. We all want to be well liked, so we avoid slightly uncomfortable situations and hope the behavior goes away. Unfortunately, the behavior usually does not just go away, and as a result, something that was not a very big deal becomes a huge issue at review time, six months later. Simply being honest with a colleague can prevent a lot of frustration and disappointment. When issues arise, talking about them immediately is absolutely critical to good Team Equity.

One of my clients told a story about being a new manager. She had a great team that worked well together. One woman on the team, however, liked to listen to a radio at her desk. It began to distract the other team members, who complained to one another about it. Finally, they came to the manager and asked her to tell the radio listener to turn it down. Our client admitted that she wasn't very experienced as a manager and figured she'd better handle the situation.

When the manager called the woman into her office and mentioned that the radio was a problem, at first the woman misunderstood! She assured her manager that listening to music helped her concentrate. When the new manager then clarified that her teammates were complaining and distracted, the woman was completely hurt. Her response was, "Why didn't they just tell me to turn it down?" Our client summed up, "I realized then that I should have told the team to do just that. The efficiency and camaraderie of the team really suffered after that event."

This may seem like a tiny issue, but it perfectly illustrates the importance of telling it like it is. What if one of the radio listener's colleagues had simply leaned over and said, "Hey, we know you like your radio, but it's distracting us. Can you turn it down, or maybe listen to it just in the morning?" The woman would have understood immediately and the small issue would have been resolved. Instead, because the team was too uncomfortable to make a simple move, the radio issue got worse and irritated them more, and weeks later this poor woman was sitting in her manager's office wondering if she was about to be reprimanded—for something she could have rectified ages before.

Another point this story beautifully illustrates is the importance of peer coaching. In a group emulating Team Equity, people are honest with each other and they are willing to help one another get better, develop, and think. For some reason, many people believe that only a manager or human resources representative should give developmental advice, but advice, notes, and honesty happen all the time in truly high-performing teams. As a result, there is constant improvement and people trust that their colleagues come to them with positive intent. If more tough information is handled simply, immediately, and honestly, teams can more easily practice Team Equity.

Team Equity and Bunnies:
It's about How You Show Up

There's an exercise called Bunny Bunny that I've facilitated hundreds of times with corporate teams. And yes, it does involve people acting like bunnies. Believe it—I've had CEOs of Fortune 500 companies, vice presidents in charge of millions of dollars of profit and sales, and buttoned-up senior partners play this game with gusto. There are some key rules to this game:

- A bunny must be formed by three people working together. One person pantomimes the teeth of the bunny with his or her hands in front of the mouth, and the two people on either side use their hands to create big ears on top of the middle person's head. They all shout "Bunny, bunny, bunny!" together for as long as they are the bunny.

- The responsibility of being the bunny has to be clearly passed. When one trio is done, the middle (teeth) person must point at someone else across the circle of participants and indicate that they are the new teeth. That means the two people on either side of the new teeth are the ears, and the game continues.

- The game is not over until everyone has played. Everyone has to be part of the bunny during the game. (You may be relieved to know that there are no observers in our workshops. You play or you get out.)

When the game is over, we ask for honesty. "How did that feel?" Responses range from "Energized!" and "That was fun!" to "Completely ridiculous!" When we ask participants why they think we had them play that game, the responses again vary widely, from "To feel like idiots" to "To break down barriers and get us relaxed" to "To jump in and work together."

At this point, I begin to discuss the behaviors I've noted while facilitating the game. There's often a marked difference in the way individuals play. Some people are leaning forward, watching the game pass from one group of bunnies to the next, laughing and ready to play. Some people actually sneer or look like a deer in headlights. When the game comes to them, they wait to begin until they check with the other two people, not wanting to go it alone. After they do the minimum that the game requires, they often step back from the circle. If the bunny comes back around to them, they sometimes complain, "But I already did it!" Or worse, the bunny comes back to them but they've disengaged so completely that their colleagues have to yell to get their attention and keep the game rolling.

More than anything, this game is about how you show up for your team. Think about that. When you finish your part of a project and it's off your desk, do you check out? Sometimes we just forget about it, don't care if it goes awry elsewhere, and don't bother to make sure the handoff was clear so that the next department can manage it. And when it comes back around, you might hear yourself saying, "But I already had it!"

It's time to take a good look at our own behavior. Team Equity and high performance are about being focused on the game at hand. If you stand back, do the minimum required, and wait for it to be over, or if you don't step out until you're sure other people are coming with you, you are a weak link. For your own growth, you deserve to be a bigger part of the game, and your team needs you.

In every work environment, people tend to know who the leaders and the get-it-doners are. In Bunny Bunny, it only takes one committed person to elevate the entire game. If just one person in a huge circle steps up, doesn't hold back, comes up with a more creative way to make a bunny with three people, then cheers on colleagues as they track the progress of the game, the team is transformed.

We all have a choice every day about how we show up. Have you ever noticed that a person's attitude or energy can affect everyone around them? We have the choice to lift ourselves and our teams up or to bring them down.

In addition to your tendency to either elevate or push down the people around you, Bunny Bunny illustrates another factor: discomfort. Adults like to be comfortable; however, the most important thing we can do to develop and learn is to allow ourselves to be uncomfortable. Stepping out of a circle of colleagues and acting like a bunny elicits a huge amount of discomfort! It also teaches you to stop being afraid of something you've never done, especially if your team is there to support you. There will be many days in your professional life when you'll feel like a complete idiot, doing something totally new and really hoping that your team is there to back you up. Recognize that you have more skills than are listed on your résumé, listen, direct your focus to the challenge at hand, and you will greatly increase your chances for success.

When I went into network engineering sales with only an education in humanities and theater, I felt ridiculous more days than not. But I brought to the table communication and collaboration skills that my engineering colleagues did not have, and that improved our team as a whole. With Team Equity, as long as you've been supportive in your colleagues' moments of exploration, there's a good chance they'll be there for you. As a result, you can trust both yourself and your colleagues in moments when you feel as silly as a bunny. Pretty soon, with ample preparation and experience, tough situations feel easier.

⁕ The secret is to work less as individuals and more as a team. As a coach, I play not my eleven best but my best eleven.

KNUTE ROCKNE

We all like to work within our circle of comfort, where we are smart, capable, and don't have to strain ourselves. But when we move outside that circle, we move into a place where our learning curve accelerates exponentially.

One of the best comments I ever heard after Bunny Bunny came from a senior partner at a top global accounting firm. The firm has a great practice of mixing very senior leaders with campus hires during the first week of training. My ensemble was conducting workshops for several ballrooms full of eager new hires, and the example of successful, playful partners aided our efforts immensely.

After playing Bunny Bunny with a circle of new people, this senior leader really got it. He looked at the young recruits and said, "I've been with the firm for over twenty years, and a partner for sixteen years. There's always something new I have to learn or something I've never encountered before. After all these years, I still feel like I'm Bunny Bunny-ing every day! It's one of the best parts of my job."

Team Equity on a Shrinking Globe

As we consider the critical importance of Team Equity to the profitability and sustainability of any organization, it's time to embrace the fact that diversity is the most profitable choice we can make. The word *diversity* has become unfortunately loaded with all sorts of negative connotations. It's been condensed, in many minds, to refer only to race or cultural background. For some people, it's connected to the thought of legal obligations and a sense of shame.

Diversity is a business imperative. With the advent of global travel, global business, social networking, and technology, we never again need to be confined to our street, city, or region. Almost anyone can engage in a global conversation. And as the baby boomers retire, we are in desperate need of more talent. If we do not hire and promote everywhere we can, there will not be enough people to do the work required.

Diversity of gender, cultural background, race, religion, sexual orientation, military status, disabled status, family status, age, and education all are elements of a diverse team.

When there is diversity across multiple dimensions, there is diversity of thought, capability, and skill. This creates a healthy tension between information and innovation, which in turn increases the possibility for real results.

Thankfully, research continues to prove that diversity supports the bottom line. For instance, Roy D. Adler of Pepperdine University did an extensive nineteen-year study of gender diversity among 215 Fortune 500 firms. His work showed "a strong correlation between a strong record of promoting women into the executive suite and high profitability." Using three measures of profitability, Adler demonstrated that "the twenty-five Fortune 500 firms with the best record of promoting women to high positions are between 18 and 69 percent more profitable than the median Fortune 500 firms in their industries."[4]

Let us also consider the advantage of reflecting our clients' diversity. I worked with a director at a global professional services firm, a man so pumped about the advantages of Team Equity he could hardly hold it in. He told us, "The diversity of my team wins deals on a day-to-day basis. I can literally watch them outstrip our competitors." I asked him to elaborate.

His team includes people native to China, Germany, Kenya, Japan, Poland, and Puerto Rico. When they get a request from a client in any of those regions, the director sticks his head out of his office, calls a colleague, and is literally speaking the client's language in moments. His competitors have to hang up, call an office in that region, wait for a response, and get back to the client a day or two later. And that's not even the biggest advantage. His team also has taught him to be sensitive to clients' religious holidays and to the family responsibilities they may have, and to understand their sensibilities in order to best do business with them.

He said that the biggest surprise came to him one day when one of his team members gave him a metaphorical smack on the forehead. She'd been on the team for five months and the director wanted to be sure she was feeling comfortable and was able to do her work. He asked her if it was tough to be the only African-American female on the team. She laughed and answered, "Tim, you're the biggest minority on the team. You're the only single parent! I'm doing just great. The question is, how are you coping during this busy time?" He said that getting a better perspective on himself that day was a great gift.

Diversity is a perfect encapsulation of equity not equality. The more diverse the team, the more dimensions available, the more flexible the team can be. The team has more skills and experiences to rely upon when the unexpected occurs.

Team Equity Case Study:
Change at Coca-Cola Enterprises

Like most big enterprises, Coca-Cola Enterprises has a large information technology department. The division, known as Business Information Services (BIS), had a history of promoting from within, so some of its chief information officers had started out as Coke truck drivers or came from merchandising or manufacturing. This is a great thing, if the individual can manage the demands and complexity of such a high-level leadership position. Unfortunately for BIS, in several cases the promoted individuals were not ideal technology leaders. This left BIS with a legacy of outdated, complicated, slow technology and no place at the decision-making table of the Coke business.

This situation is not unique. Information technology departments at large enterprises often are treated as service organizations that should do as they're told, and they often are not consulted as part of a business decision.

That is roughly the position in which Coca-Cola Enterprises' BIS found itself in 2006. It had more than six hundred fifty applications across multiple platforms. It had a warehouse management system that was impossible to install and was working in only two of six hundred warehouses. A long run of chief information officers who came from finance or human resources allowed expensive consultants to manage most of the high-level work, and 80 percent of internal information technology resources were focused on just maintaining the status quo for Coca-Cola Enterprises. Capital expenditures were through the roof.

Then, something rather amazing happened. From 2006 to 2010, an unexpected leadership change took place at Coca-Cola Enterprises, and part of that wave was the appointment of Y. Esat Sezer as chief information officer at BIS. His story and his accomplishments in three short years are a model of Team Equity.

The board of Coca-Cola Enterprises knew it had to do something about its enterprise in early 2006. So for the first time in the company's history, an outside CEO was hired. John Brock came to a tough job, and the first thing he did was reassess his own direct reports. Brock had spent twenty-three years in the beverage industry, and if there was one talent upon which he relied, it was his singular ability to size up people quickly.

He conducted interviews and assessments of about seventy-five people during his first few weeks as CEO. He knew that he wanted immediate changes in several functions, beginning with human resources and information technology. Brock considers human resources and information technology to be strategic weapons in any large enterprise. If they're not run well, you don't have a chance. If you have great leadership, you have at least half a chance. Brock needed strong information technology leadership with double capabilities: strong technical competence paired with executive presence and a full understanding of the business. Unfortunately, in his experience, he usually encountered techno-geeks who couldn't speak to laypeople or managers who had learned a bunch of technology terms and sounded good but had no real technical capabilities. As Brock explained, "When I met Esat, I knew I had found that rare combination of double talent."

Brock hired Sezer in October 2006 and gave him an unbelievable challenge: to transform, consolidate, and simplify the Coca-Cola Enterprises infrastructure, and to lower operating and capital expenditures so that it could show profit and value for Coca-Cola's shareholders.

"And, oh yeah," he told Sezer, "do it in three years."

Sezer recalls how daunting the challenge seemed. He had an impressive track record in global information technology transformations but he had never been asked to accomplish one with such speed. Yet, in the course of just three years, Sezer employed improvisational skills that allowed him to standardize six platforms rather than six hundred fifty, eliminate expensive consultants, and return the fun, interesting work to his internal talent. He outsourced boring, repetitive work and created almost $70 million of value for shareholders through a systematic reduction of operating and capital expenses. Wow!

And the first thing this leader will tell you? "We succeeded as a team."

Sezer and the BIS team met their challenges by employing the three attributes of Team Equity: own it, equity not equality, and tell it like it is.

Owning It at Coca-Cola Enterprises

One factor in Sezer's decision to take the job at Coca-Cola Enterprises was the simple fact that he'd be reporting directly to the CEO. That ensured that his work would be visible and his decisions final. He was owning it like an improviser in the middle of the stage. He *wanted* to be the one responsible for the changes. He was going to see this thing through, and the buck stopped with him.

He also was willing to stand by his decisions and make compromises on the outcomes of his team's work—a key part of improvisational flexibility. Pam Kimmet, senior vice president of human resources, is one of Sezer's peers on the executive team. She gave an example of his flexibility in owning it: Sezer had made the decision to standardize on a platform that Kimmet had never used. She disagreed because she had used another platform in multiple organizations over the previous fifteen years. However, Sezer stood his ground and promised Kimmet that the platform would do everything she needed it to do for her own aggressive goals in growing and developing Coca-Cola Enterprises' talent. Kimmet said, "I trusted him and he really came through for me. He made sure that the platform performed on every metric I demanded, and made sure that my team could use it efficiently."

＊ Talent wins games. But teamwork and intelligence win championships.

MICHAEL JORDAN

When I interviewed Kimmet, I did not tell her that the underlying concept of this book is trust. So it was incredibly gratifying when, as she discussed the improvisational behaviors of the BIS team, she continually brought up trust.

"Esat made huge deposits, over time, into what I think of as a trust bank. He acted consistently both in good and bad times," she recounted. That trust was built because he emulated the improv behavior of owning it.

Sezer also spent considerable time and energy getting the right people into place and then letting *them* own it. Brock mentioned that one of the ways that Sezer first established trust was through the people he presented for hire. Whenever Sezer wanted to bring in new talent, he asked

Brock to interview them. Without exception, his choices were excellent.

Brenda Whipple, a sourcing expert in Sezer's organization, said, "Whenever we go into negotiations with vendors, we know that Esat has put responsibility entirely into our hands. We own it, and he has our back. Some vendors like to play a game where they go around the negotiation team and speak with the [chief information officer] to pull favors. Not once has Esat made a side deal or overturned our work."

Whipple mentioned that, after coming from a career of frustration caused by that sort of behavior, it has been incredible to be able to do her job and know that she has the support of her leader. Her team is able to negotiate great contracts, and she feels her work is respected.

Equity Not Equality at Coca-Cola Enterprises

The practice of applying equity not equality to teams builds trust by demanding people who are talented and engaged. To that end, the BIS review structure was changed to a high-performance team model, which meant extreme honesty in differentiation. Previously, people were ranked according to their tenure or given good marks if others on their team had good marks. Now, people were held accountable for their own performance and were ranked according to competence, results, teamwork, and communication skills. For people who wanted straight talk and improvement, this was great. For people who thought "fairness" meant keeping the status quo, it hurt.

BIS moved to an equity not equality review system. The BIS leadership team identified talent and reskilled and repositioned people, enabling them to take roles that stretched them. That continuous focus on the right team made the rest of Coca-Cola Enterprises respect and trust BIS. As Sezer commented, "If you make the right choices on talent, it becomes very clear to the organization that you mean business."

Within the first year, that talent was put to the test several times. Although the BIS management team believed certain systems were in place and had been installed correctly, they learned the hard way that their predecessors had not done a good job. Two major information technology catastrophes occurred, creating wasteful outages. BIS employed Team Equity to manage the crisis, kept people working, and created backup systems in real time. Those crises actually made BIS stronger and smarter.

Telling It Like It Is at Coca-Cola Enterprises

Great teams that emulate the principles of improvisation must share relevant information. Sezer didn't patronize his group by keeping financials and issues to himself. He shared the good, bad, ugly, and beautiful alike. This kept the team informed and invested, and his honesty built trust. Sezer tells it like it is.

However, that honesty was pretty jarring for some. If a bad decision had been made, Sezer did not mince words. Some of his current direct reports remember the culture shock they went through in 2006. Sezer was straightforward and direct and did not play political games. This was a huge change.

Mike Wright, a twenty-six-year veteran, remembers a defining moment during Sezer's first year, when Wright stood up for an individual who was under scrutiny in a meeting. It represented a serious confrontation with his chief information officer and Wright was sure that he would be fired. Instead, the individual was kept on, due to Wright's recommendation, and Wright became a trusted part of the executive BIS team.

Sezer wanted clear communication, even if it was argumentative. Business needed to get out on the table during meetings so that work could get done, and Sezer wanted his team to push back and show its strengths. It was the beginning of an open, responsive culture that rewarded telling it like it is.

Sezer also remembered that telling it like it is applied to himself. He opened an anonymous e-mail line directly to his desk, where people could air any concern without fear of retribution. He kept his calendar open for walk-ins from eight to ten o'clock every morning, and he continues that practice to this day.

In the beginning, most of the comments arrived anonymously. But Sezer honored the comments, good or bad. He listened and then he acted on the feedback. That demonstrated that he truly wanted open communication and would not punish people for having a different opinion. In fact, he values those opinions. Now he gets very few anonymous e-mails; most people speak to Sezer directly.

Coca-Cola Enterprises Keeps Improvising

Sezer's final comments were the most compelling: "I knew we could do it once I saw the vision come to life for the team. They were completely committed, personally, to achieving these goals, and then exceeded expectations! I never could have done all this without this team. We did it, and now we're setting new goals."

In 2009, ImprovEdge facilitated a celebratory conference of one hundred twenty members of the Coca-Cola Enterprises BIS leadership team. They learned about the concept of Team Equity after they had been living it. And that foundation of trust, that strength, has given them the confidence to put another aggressive three-year plan in place.

So this seems like a great place to wrap up the story, doesn't it? However, there's another surprise. In December 2009, right after the leadership conference, Brock again called Sezer with a challenge. He revealed that Coca-Cola Enterprises and the Coca-Cola Company were in confidential talks to merge their North American operations. Everything was about to change. Without a hitch, Sezer replied, "Got it. Now what do you want me to do?"

Brock replied, "You're going to have to undo everything you've worked on for the last three years. You've created a totally integrated, global IT system that runs perfectly across two continents. Now I need you to break it apart to support the new structure that will emerge from the change. And, oh yeah, let's get it done by October 1, 2010."

Words that have been used to describe the improvisational behaviors of BIS during this new transition have included *adaptable, solution focused, flexible, relentless, driven,* and *resilient.* Every action that built a foundation of trust for BIS over the past three years is serving them well during the merger.

Sezer and his team will get it done, and then some. In the words of Brock, the improvisational behaviors have been "nothing short of remarkable."

On a funny side note, it seems inevitable that Sezer would emulate improvisational behaviors. The man who put this all into action is named Yahya Esat Sezer. Y.E.S., for short.

Team Equity Behaviors

Now it's time to think about the most basic behaviors we could put into place to practice Team Equity. These are simple things you can do right now, today, to have a more high-performing team.

＊ Own it.
Show up at work! Act as if this is going to be the most important day of your career. Be positive, be collaborative, and be engaged.

＊ Equity not equality.
Ask your colleagues what they believe is their biggest strength in their work. You will learn surprising things about the talents of your team, and there may be ways to realign work so that those strengths are best leveraged.

＊ Tell it like it is.
Ask for immediate feedback on your work. Serve as an example of what it means to continually, honestly improve.

Team Equity Exercise

Meetings that Matter[5]

Here's an exercise you can engage in to make Team Equity a part of your world. It's critical to make the most of group experiences, and these tips will assist you in creating a more focused, fun, engaged meeting time. Try just one of the ideas at a time, until you and your team become used to mixing it up. Use it with your colleagues, at your place of worship, with your friends or family. Remember, Margaret Mead once said, "Never doubt that a small group of thoughtful, committed citizens can change the world. Indeed, it is the only thing that ever has."

When they work well, meetings are meant to build teamwork, generate ideas, and create consensus. Unfortunately, they're not always as positive and productive as we would like. Use these ideas to turn meetings around by turning observers into participants whose time and ideas are valued. Meetings might even become fun to attend.

Get Ready

1. Hold your meeting anywhere except a conference room
   or a place that serves food. Choose different departments for your meetings, go outside, or perhaps try
   the lobby.

2. Remove tables and other barriers from the room. Set
   chairs in a circle or in any configuration that's condu-
   cive to teamwork.

Get Set

3. Arrange for other people to present part of the meeting.
   Give them responsibilities and allow them time to prepare. Be positive about their contributions.

4. Turn off all pagers, phones, and laptops.

5. After the first break, ask everyone to change seats. Do
   this as often as is necessary. If energy levels wane,
   change places. You'll begin to see things from a different point of view.

Go

6. At the beginning of the meeting, have everyone share
   something that recently went well at work. At the end
   of the meeting, have everyone commit to an action
   based on the meeting.

7. Power down PowerPoint. Put your ideas on big sheets of paper and give everyone a different colored marker. As the meeting progresses, everyone is responsible for editing and adding to the working document.

Chapter Four

The Fourth Secret of Improvisation

Oops to Eureka!

Your last troupe member, who has not been involved up to this point, comes to the front of the stage and translates the whole song into sign language. The audience already is roaring, but this new addition really makes them scream.

There are slight lulls between verses of the songs, and just a minute after the sign language translator has come forward, a woman in the front row stands up to leave. In one of the lulls, everyone can clearly hear her say, "This is stupid. He's faking. To make fun of sign language this way is offensive. I'm leaving."

The whole audience stops laughing as she struggles to get down the aisle. Your troupe member is unsure how to finish the song, and the wind has gone out of the performance. It's like a train wreck. Suddenly, you leap forward and go down on your knee in front of the woman trying to leave.

"I beseech you: save us from this horribly translated foreign film! I'm not a cannibal; I'm just badly translated! Save the day and be our translator! We never meant to offend anyone. Please help us do this right."

The woman blushes and her eyes grow wide as the spotlight hits her. She looks around, and someone in the seat next to her says, "You can do it! Go on!"

You keep eye contact, smile, and nod encouragingly. She smiles a little, so you take her hand and help her onstage. She swallows hard and then goes over to the sign language guy. He steps back in deference and says to her, "So what is he really?"

The woman from the audience considers and says, "He's Farmer Rutabaga, who wants to take the little salad leaves and plant them to show his love for Boston Lettuce." As she says this, she signs it perfectly in actual American Sign Language.

The audience applauds and the troupe changes the song to a love ballad. Farmer Rutabaga sings of his plan to grow little lettuces with his new darling, Boston Lettuce. The woman from the audience signs the entire song and even takes a bow at the end, to wild applause.

The final and probably scariest concept of improvisation is called Oops to Eureka!, and it means knowing you're OK, even if you screw up.

Your improv troupe just experienced the unexpected. In this instance, the unexpected occurrence was also a train wreck—when something goes terribly wrong with the performance. You know it, your troupe knows it, and the audience knows it. Oops to Eureka! insists that we examine our mistakes rather than running from them, and that we use them as an opportunity.

In improv, the best moments onstage often come right after a train wreck. That's because people are impressed if you can do something brilliant with a mess. Improv makes fixing a train wreck both tough and easy. It's tough because, unlike scripted work, where you can move to another scripted point or rely on someone offstage to fix the wreck, the entire improv team is onstage and you all have to fix it in the moment. On the other hand, fixing a train wreck is easy because it is improv—if you follow the secrets, agree and collaborate, a solution can be created in the moment.

✳ Eureka! ("I have found it!")

ARCHIMEDES[1]

However, oops does not refer to only problems or mistakes. The unexpected is not necessarily bad, and it often shows up in a pleasant way: a business request from a client you have not heard from in more than a year, an answer to a problem, or flowers when it is not your birthday.

✳ Out of chatter, find simplicity. From discord, find harmony. In the middle of difficulty lies opportunity.

ALBERT EINSTEIN

Isaac Asimov was once quoted as saying, "The most exciting phrase to hear in science, the one that heralds new discoveries, is not 'Eureka!' (I found it!) but 'That's funny . . .'" It is the incongruous, the surprise, the thing that makes us furrow our brow and look closer that eventually leads to the eureka moment. It's our job to cultivate the curiosity of a scientist, mixed with the playfulness of an improviser. That incredibly effective mix, which is the cornerstone of innovation, is Oops to Eureka!.

There are specific components to cultivating this excellent Oops to Eureka! capability. The components of managing the unexpected, the Oops to Eureka! moments, are:

✳ See it and say it

✳ Flip it

✳ Use it

See It and Say It

To handle the unexpected like an improviser, you first have to recognize and acknowledge the incident. See it and say it demands that you be both aware and courageous in the moment the unexpected occurs. In 1862, Friedrich August Kekulé reportedly had a dream about a snake seizing its own tail. He had spent more than seven years studying the nature of carbon-carbon bonds, a great puzzle to scientists at the time. After his strange dream, Kekulé connected the image with his scientific ponderings and realized he could describe the structure of benzene—which is shaped like a ring or a snake biting its tail. Many other people, even scientists, would have said, "What a weird dream" and gone on with their day. Kekulé saw it and said it. He made his idea public at a conference, and his hypothesis ultimately was proved in 1929.

3M made a big mistake with an adhesive. Spencer Silver, a scientist in the 3M research labs, wanted to create a strong bond for paper. However, the adhesive he created just didn't stick well; it peeled right off. Oops! The scientist shelved the product. About four years later, another 3M scientist, Arthur Fry, was singing in his church choir. He was annoyed when his hymnal markers kept falling out and he suddenly remembered the weak adhesive his colleague had invented. He applied some of the adhesive to his hymnal markers and discovered that they could be applied and removed without causing damage to the pages. Post-it Notes became 3M's most successful product. Eureka!

As in our improv scene example, it may be an outside

force—in that case, a disgruntled audience member—that appears as the unexpected or uncomfortable event. In the workplace, the catalyst might be any of a million unexpected occurrences—a client goes bankrupt, a new colleague joins the team, a flight is canceled, a customer nominates you for an award.

In the vegetable scene, everyone in the house was willing to run with the scene as it was set up, except for one vocal, offended person. The audience was affected by the strength of her feelings, embarrassed for the troupe onstage, and uncertain as a group how to respond. They froze as an audience. Everyone knew that there was an incongruous event. Everyone saw it. But was someone going to say it?

The troupe could have ignored the incident, let the woman leave, and gone on with the show. However, in order to move beyond oops, you've got to say it. And that takes guts.

The key ingredient in saving the show was the acknowledgment of the oops. Having the courage to admit that something is unusual, messed up, or different is beyond admirable. It is a key attribute of great leaders, great teams, and great achievers. In many instances, knowing there is an incongruity is not too hard. But *saying* there is an incongruity, having the courage to admit it, represents an amazing step forward.

When I was a young teen, I saw my first production of the play *Talley's Folly*. Not knowing the script, I thought it seemed strange when the male lead put his foot through the dock early in the play. He seemed very flustered, out of character, and there was a long silence onstage. He and the female lead exchanged weird glances and went on with the play.

It wasn't until the end of the play, when the actor put his leg through the dock again, that I realized the first incident had been a mistake. The action that elicited no response from the actors in the first half suddenly was a huge problem in the second half. The female lead said, "Oh, my goodness, are you hurt?" and then they went on with the script.

In that moment in the first half when an accident occurred, a big elephant appeared in the room and everybody saw it. Unfortunately, the actors succumbed to their discomfort and punted the entire production by ignoring it—by refusing to say it.

The phrase "elephant in the room" refers to an issue or occurrence that is affecting everyone but that no one will talk about. Think about how ridiculous it would seem to have an elephant standing in your conference room during a meeting but having no one acknowledge it! The elephant in the room is usually the most important thing on everyone's mind. It's uncomfortable and it stifles people's ability to focus or communicate because they're all obsessed with the unspoken reality. I've worked with corporate teams and executives who have been existing through days, weeks, and months during which unspoken issues kill their ability to focus and engage. Yet, because of politics, hierarchy, or fear, no one will raise the real issue—no one will say it.

In negotiation, this happens when no one will address the one uncomfortable thing that will get the deal done. For example, I was involved in a bid for ethics and compliance training. Everyone knew the organization we were pitching had to have the training because it was under scrutiny and facing potential legal action due to ethics and compliance problems. I knew that the other suppliers were talking about their processes and benefits, their pricing and execution, and probably not saying anything directly to the committee about the organization's difficult situation. But the big question in the client's mind was really whether this training would help change the behavior in its culture and protect it from future incidents.

So my ensemble and I acted like improvisers. The first thing we said was, "We know you are in potential litigation right now for ethics and compliance offenses on the employee level. That's a scary place to be, and we want to address how our training will teach better behaviors and create a system of coverage should a future incident occur."

That was extremely risky. We could have offended any number of people and gotten ourselves tossed out of the room. Instead, we got the deal, and there have been no further issues to date for that client.

Let's be realistic, though. The acknowledgment of an elephant in the room does not always have a rosy outcome. We were working with a management team that was suffering from the verbally inappropriate and offensive behavior of a few of its members. They were leaders, and my ensemble was seriously worried that they could cause employee harassment issues. Everyone could see it. Human resources had even slapped a wrist or two, but the overarching response was to act like it was a small nonissue.

So, we said it. We told it like it was in the hope that we

could inspire the team to take positive action. Instead, we were fired from the account. This was the right thing for the client to do, considering the explosive nature of the situation and our putting it on the table. We knew we were taking a risk, and we were well aware of that possible consequence. We probably should have handled it more delicately, and my ensemble and I learned a lot from that experience, but there was a real reaction of relief among the members of the client team who had been persevering through the bad behavior. Somebody had finally just said it. Many months later, the managers engaging in inappropriate behavior were subject to disciplinary action.

The actors in *Talley's Folly* could have adjusted to the mistake; they could have discussed the terrible upkeep of the dock and warned one another to be careful. They could have moved the next scene to another part of the stage while they administered first aid. So many improvised solutions could have made the whole play seem complete and OK to the audience. But they punted and didn't say it. They froze up and went along with the script.

Your improv troupe in the vegetable scene, by contrast, acknowledged its mistake and started to look for ways to make it not only workable but also brilliant. And that's where *flip it* comes in.

Flip It

The act of flipping it when you encounter the unexpected is often a mental moment. It involves training the brain to see something as an opportunity rather than a problem.

This requires a flexibility that needs to be practiced. Going to plan B is not always our preference. When it rains on the one day you have for the beach on your vacation, it can be a very difficult thing to flip. But this click in your brain has to occur if eureka is ever going to happen.

It's really as simple as having a mantra: "Something unexpected has happened. I don't really like it or want it. And how I choose to think about it will determine whether I flip this thing or not. I'm going to spend a minute just thinking about how this could be an opportunity."

In all honesty, not every incongruous event turns into something great, and tough lessons sometimes stay tough. But coming at an issue with the improviser's mind-set, with the scientist's mind-set, can transform how you and your team handle the unexpected and reap its benefits.

⁕ Experience should teach us that it is always the unexpected that does occur.

ELEANOR ROOSEVELT

My friend Leslie is a financial executive in an advertising firm. She stopped by my house to talk to me one evening, and I knew from the moment she stepped out of the car that something was terribly wrong. Her team had made a million-dollar mistake and she had missed the signs. By the time she got to my house, she felt physically sick. She had said it to the CEO and was in the midst of trying to figure out what to do. She knew she'd have to fire some of her team, rectify the problem with the client, beg for patience and money back from several vendors, and then maybe be fired herself. At the end of her story she looked at me and said, "In the fifteen years I've spent with this firm, I've never made such a mistake."

I nodded and let her have a moment of silence. Then I said, "And how you deal with it, Leslie, will define your next fifteen years with the firm." She looked at me in a surprised way, but almost immediately I saw a light come on in her eyes. I told her about a bit of advice I once heard from an extremely successful angel investor, John Huston: the size of the problems you solve determines the size of the paycheck you receive.

"Leslie," I said, "you're going to fix this. You already have a plan in place to rectify the event. Now I want you to think about how this can be a springboard to improve the firm's processes and elevate your status. I remember you once told me you'd love to reimagine many of the processes your company uses but that no one would invest the time or capital. If changing those processes could not only prevent another event but also create new financial opportunity and cut expenses, this could be your big chance to present that plan to the CEO. Don't think of this as the end. Think of it as the beginning."

Leslie went in swinging. She focused her confidence, clarity, and determination. Not only did she keep her own job but also her plan allowed her to keep most of her team intact and to roll out the new processes.

The unexpected may look like a box wrapped in stinky fish paper, covered with slimy goo and dirt. And you can decide to judge that book by its cover. But if you have the courage to flip it, you just might find that the underside of the box is a work of art.

✳ A life spent making mistakes is not only more honorable but more useful than a life spent doing nothing.

GEORGE BERNARD SHAW

Use It

Improvisational eureka demands that everything be recognized and justified. In the improviser's mind-set, mistakes have to be acknowledged and dealt with immediately. Even mistakes deserve a moment onstage. If you wait too long and try to go back to fix it later in the performance, it's often no longer relevant, and you've lost the interest of the audience—a terrible performer's sin.

In the vegetable scene, it was in that moment of extreme discomfort, when the woman spoke up and tried to leave the theater, that you, the improviser, saw it, said it, flipped it, and trusted yourself to take a great risk and use it. You asked an audience member to come up onstage! No one expected that to happen, and it was a risky solution. There are at least a million other ways that this sort of risk could have gone, many of them not so pretty.

When working onstage in an art as fluid and uncertain as improvisation, improvisers learn that the unexpected will be a regular part of the work. Mistakes, blips, missed cues, unacknowledged moments, and crazy opportunities all are part of the trade. Improvisers become so used to encountering them, managing them, and turning them around that the unexpected starts to lose most of its scariness. Somehow, knowing that these irregularities are unavoidable makes it easier to deal with them. It becomes a sport to see just how well improvisers can handle tough situations, how they can create a fabulous eureka out of an unexpected oops moment. In some really impressive troupes, I've seen members throw insane curve balls at their team members, just to keep them on their toes. Of course, this means they are open to being messed with on the same level, and it elevates the whole show.

✳ Jazz is just riffing on your mistakes.

ORNETTE COLEMAN

On an improv stage, nothing can be ignored. I recently went to a college improv performance featuring one of my interns. She was brilliant. She also made the mistake of saying something under her breath about her scene partner. There was no way her fellow improvisers were going to let that slide. One member who was offstage actually made himself the narrator and called her on it. Not only that, but he also demanded that she move into the light on the lip of the stage and sing a song about the sexual tension between herself and the other guy onstage. Yowza! Now that's truth. Granted, it was also funny. That's why we love comedy and improv. It's cathartic.

And it worked so well because one actor saw it and said it, my intern flipped what he handed her, and they used it. Even though the two of them were messing with each other, they knew they could push each other. He trusted that she would answer his call to sing, no matter how tough it was. She knew the risk and reward of doing so. She also trusted that he'd join her onstage if she faltered. Their ultimate goal was to keep the audience surprised, delighted, and engaged. They more than achieved their goal.

My friend Leslie from the advertising firm used her million-dollar oops and ended up with a eureka. Likewise, one of Marie Curie's experiments failed during her research. She saw it and said it, and as she was headed out to dispose of the mess, decided to flip it a bit. She used it and spent some extra time examining the result. She discovered radium that day.

Theodor S. Geisel's first children's book was rejected by twenty-three publishers. The twenty-fourth publisher sold six million copies. He's better known today as Dr. Seuss.

Everyone remembers that Babe Ruth hit 714 home runs. But do you know how many times he struck out during the regular season? 1,330. He said, "Every time I strike out, I get that much closer to my next home run."

Recently, when we were working with a state realtors association, I gave a speech about the four secrets of improv and told the Babe Ruth story. One of the most successful real estate agents in the group pulled me aside during the break to show me his business card case. Engraved on the inside was the number 1,330. He really gets it.

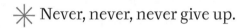 Never, never, never give up.

WINSTON CHURCHILL

Sometimes Oops Is Tiny

Even very small, incongruous events can change huge things. Ruth Wakefield thought she had ruined her chocolate cookies for her guests at the Toll House Inn. She had thrown in pieces of chocolate without melting them first, and when the lumpy, chunk-filled cookies came out of the oven, they looked like a mistake. Her guests soon assured her she had stumbled on the best cookie they'd ever eaten. The chocolate chip cookie became America's number one cookie and Nestlé now has a multimillion-dollar product based on that first batch of "ruined" cookies.

I was on a plane back home from a business trip when, during some unexpected turbulence, the flight attendant lost her balance and spilled hot coffee on my leg. Oops. It hurt a lot and I had to apply ice for a while. Although the flight attendant helped me, no one around me even mentioned the spill. Instead, they ignored it, perhaps to avoid embarrassing me further. I really didn't care, and I've always found it interesting that spills and messes can be more embarrassing for people who witness the event than for those who experience it.

As I disembarked and headed for the baggage claim, a man tapped me on the shoulder. He mentioned that he'd been in the aisle across from me, had seen the accident, and wanted to know if I was OK. He said it, rather than ignoring it. I assured him all was fine, and thanked him.

We chatted about the weather and little things as we went to the baggage area. He mentioned that he'd been at a convention for ideation and creativity. I asked him about it and he had a lot of interesting things to say about the experience. I realized there was an unexpected opportunity here, so I decided to flip it. I took a small risk. I told him about my company, our work in creativity and ideation, and offered him my card. I wanted to use this unexpected conversation as a marketing opportunity. I asked him to check out our Web site if he had the chance. He politely accepted, we said good-bye, and I promptly forgot about the whole incident.

A few days later, I received an e-mail. It turns out that he was a leader in his organization and he and his team wanted to talk about our work in corporate creativity and ideation. That organization became one of our biggest clients. Eureka!

In some cases, a spill of hot coffee could really ruin your day. In this case, it was the unexpected occurrence that opened a door I never would have seen otherwise.

Oops to Eureka! Case Study:
Computers for Youth Atlanta

Computers for Youth (CFY) in Atlanta, Georgia, has been displaying an improvisational mind-set since its inception.[2] CFY is a nationwide nonprofit organization that helps low-income children perform better in school by improving their home learning environments. The signature program helps educators to build stronger home-school connections and provides families with the key ingredients required to improve home learning, including providing free computers for home use. Families are invited to attend half-day workshops that not only show them how to use the donated computers but also demonstrate how parents can help their children to learn.

CFY targets schools in which at least 75 percent of students are eligible for free or reduced-price lunches. Studies of the CFY program confirm that it has significantly improved students' test scores and class effort and has increased parents' confidence.

With true improvisational positivity, Elizabeth Stock, CEO and cofounder of CFY, has built an organization that focuses on assets rather than on deficits. "We don't focus on what our clients may be lacking. We focus on what they *do* have, such as a unique background or a curious mind. In the same manner, we prefer to see our own positive assets at CFY, such as a great culture and driven staff, rather than what we may lack—such as an endowment." In addition, Bheesham Sethi, a CFY executive, notes CFY's solid Oops to Eureka! mind-set: "We've created a safe culture here. Our people can make mistakes and know that it will be all right. Mistakes are how we learn and get better."

I learned about this culture from the executive director of the Atlanta branch of CFY, Jeanne Artime. She calls it "the day we went up in flames but still came out a phoenix." CFY Atlanta knows hardship and unexpected difficulty. But more than that, it knows Oops to Eureka!, because when the organization faces a challenge it also finds a reason to learn, celebrate, and move on.

Seeing It and Saying It at Computers for Youth

CFY Atlanta grew. It thrived. Then, on Saturday, November 8, 2008, Artime found herself in the halls of a middle school waiting to start an important day. In tandem with her partner, Richard Hicks, her team was going to be teaching more than one hundred twenty families to use a computer—everything from plugging it in to using the software—and then loading up the machines so that the families could take them home.

The setup requires a lot of logistical preparation: two sessions of about sixty families each (one in the morning and one in the afternoon, each with as many as one hundred fifty people), four classrooms with three rows of five computers each, one family trainer at the front of each room, multiple volunteers moving through each classroom to help with questions and troubleshooting, at least five on-site technical assistants, and several logistics and registration volunteers.

In addition, the schools in which CFY Atlanta works often are in poor shape and may not have good electrical resources. CFY plans for this. On that November day, the technical team had extra orange power cords and power strips as well as extra computers in case some malfunctioned. This was critical, because they were working in a particularly dilapidated middle school.

The first workshop began at nine o'clock. After introductions, the family trainers invited the participants to plug in and power up. And all the power went down. Oops. Then, only one row of computers in each room would power up.

The technical team and teachers immediately said to their clients, "We seem to have an issue. Hang in there and we'll get it all figured out." They saw it and said it, and in the first few moments, thought this was just another small, unexpected electrical glitch, easily fixed.

Flipping It and Using It at Computers for Youth

The technical team zoomed from seeing it and saying it right to the realization that they had to flip it. The situation was unexpected, but CFY's mission was to create a great learning environment for its clients. The trainers immediately used the outage as a way to show the families how prepared the CFY team was. The techs began switching to backup power cords. Another row of computers came online—and the first row went down. The family trainers rolled with it and kept teaching while the tech team worked. The techs would rewire and get the last row powered, only to realize that two other classrooms had lost power entirely.

At that point, everyone realized that this issue was far bigger than anything else they had dealt with. The situation also became confused because in some classrooms it was difficult to tell whether the power was failing or a computer was failing. The technical team began swapping out computers. The family trainers kept teaching. The volunteers kept offering tips and worked on keeping the class focused.

Artime, Hicks, and every other CFY person was scrambling. What was going on, and why weren't the backups filling the gaps?

Artime ran to the school's computer lab to check on the PCs there. Only about half of those were working. In the ten minutes she was gone, the tech team was able to ensure that the family trainers' computers stayed powered, but they had turned off all the family computers and were running the class on demo only. Each classroom simply could not handle fifteen computers on full power.

At that point, there was a moment of truth. "We had to ask ourselves, Is this solution acceptable?" They were in the midst of terrible hardship and difficulty, but Artime felt that using only demo was not a good solution.

If they had been on an improvisational stage, the performance would have been deemed a train wreck. The improv troupe would have had to decide whether to just limp to a conclusion of the show or to flip it and look for a totally unexpected way to save the performance. Computers for Youth had to consider whether this was the absolute best they could offer their clients.

Ultimately, the team decided that every family, every workshop, deserved the full experience. They weren't going to quit at demo mode only. They would find a way to flip this, no matter what.

At this point, some of the family trainers were dancing and telling jokes as they kept the families laughing, learning, and working.

"Richard and I and the rest of the team immediately began brainstorming. What other solutions were there?" Artime's team realized that they could spread the workshops over eight classrooms and have enough power, but there were only four family trainers, so that solution wouldn't work. They went back to the breaker box to reassess, did some math, and realized that they could rewire the box to send power from an empty classroom to the teaching classrooms. Then each teaching classroom had the power of two classrooms, which would power all the computers and monitors.

That was a real solution. They went for it and began rewiring.

By 11:45, CFY had all the computers powered up and working. They were able to get the critical hands-on components taught and practiced by the families before they packed up the computers and sent them home an hour later. Just two hours after that, another sixty families showed up for the afternoon session, which went without a hitch.

The most amazing part of this whole story is that not one family complained. The show went on, ladies and gentlemen, even when the main character, the actual computers, didn't perform. Eureka!

I asked Artime a lot of questions about the behavior of her team during that crisis, and about what they learned or changed, and her answers consistently included descriptions of improvisational behaviors. The team simply didn't stop. Not one person ever so much as rolled his eyes. Instead, they rolled up their sleeves and started patching the grid, rearranging wires and outlets, troubleshooting the different rooms. Every time the team got one line of computers working, another would go out. They experienced oops after oops after oops but the teachers, staff, and volunteers just kept saying "Yes, and," kept working together, and eventually got everything running. Failure was not an option!

Artime and Hicks both noted that there has never been finger-pointing at CFY Atlanta. No matter what kept going wrong that day, they just kept working together. It was never a matter of "You wired it wrong"; instead, it was a matter of "Something's not working. Now what do we do about it?" Although I spoke to Artime and Hicks separately, they both used the word *trust* to mark the foundation of the team's relationship.

Artime summed it up: "We certainly learned to have even more backup than before that day, but I think more than anything, we learned that we could do it. I've never been more proud of a team or more honored to work with those people than I was that day. And in an improv mind-set, we just kept saying, 'Yes, we can do this. Yes, yes, yes.'"

Ultimately, the eureka for CFY has been a realization that the organization is capable of far more than they knew. Getting through this crisis with such aplomb has filled the team with greater confidence and an understanding that their team is truly extraordinary.

I've been in many work environments where everything was going wrong. The potential loss usually involved money, client retention, legal action, or terrible distress to customers or colleagues. Despite the crisis, I've watched people throw up their hands and walk away "because it's five o'clock" or "because it's not really my responsibility." Or perhaps they settled for the barest minimum they could deliver. Thoughts like that never even crossed the minds of the CFY team.

That's an incredible thing to watch. The people at CFY all feel really lucky to be doing this work. They have a mission, something bigger than themselves, and everyone on the team cares deeply about what they do. They are there for the families, and that's the bottom line. All the CFY members I interviewed share not only a passion for their work but also an ability to employ improvisational skills every day.

CFY epitomizes a trusting, improvisational, high-performing team. The Atlanta team on-site at that electrically challenged school decided that no matter what the unexpected occurrence, they had to provide the highest level of service to the families, which meant hands-on learning using working computers. They made the choice to create a better outcome. They saw it and said it. Then they flipped it by defining the event as their most challenging opportunity to impress their clients. Finally, they used it as an opportunity to show themselves and their clients that CFY could come through, no matter what.

Discover the unexpected, rather than bemoaning it. And as you explore the concept through these next exercises, consider the words of Margaret J. Wheatley: "The things we fear most in organizations—fluctuations, disturbances, imbalances—need not be signs of an impending disorder that will destroy us. Instead, fluctuations are the primary source of creativity."[3]

Oops to Eureka! Behaviors

Here are a few simple steps for getting comfortable with discomfort. Believe me, your physical triggers will continue to show up when you hit an oops—you might perspire, blush, or feel your heart rate increase. But you'll also begin to see those signs as your body telling you that there's a eureka around the corner.

* See it and say it.
  When something unexpected occurs, pause and breathe. Try saying, "That's funny . . ." Let anyone who could be affected know about it immediately.

* Flip it.
  Once you've acknowledged it, take a minute to think about how this might create a best outcome rather than a worst one.

* Use it.
  If you've really committed to seeing it and saying it, and you've flipped it, there is no other choice than to use it. Be the first in there rather than being a follower. Suggest an alternative, spring on the opportunity, and just do it.

Oops to Eureka! Exercise

Do More with Less[4]

Improvisation is the perfect analogy for learning to live with less. Consider improv ensembles, which arrive onstage without any of the common tools of theater: no costumes, props, or scripts. And with nothing, they have to create magic. The very constraint of having less allows them to be more creative. If you're suddenly staring scarcity in the face, see it as an opportunity rather than as a punishment or a problem. You'll discover something you never considered before, and you'll make miracles out of nothing.

Get Ready

1. What is currently missing? Instead of seeing a void in your imagination, envision a door opening onto something entirely new.

2. Research, ask questions, and reverse your assumptions. What have you not considered before? If you've always used expensive advertising, for instance, what can you do for free with social media?

Get Set

3. If you are used to working with a big budget or lots of people, examine low-cost or free alternatives that may suit your needs. How do nonprofits function? What guerrilla tactics have you not explored?

4. Partner and collaborate. Can you swap services for something you need? Can you barter your goods for the expertise you are missing?

Go

5. Enjoy being free of clutter and complication. Scarcity also implies simplicity, focus, and elegance. You'll better understand the core value of yourself and your organization, and you'll see distractions for what they are.

Practice.
Then Celebrate!

Improvisers are often the most over-rehearsed people in the performance industry. That fact takes some people by surprise. But, as we've seen, improvisation is built upon preparation, skilled behaviors, and collaboration, so we should assume that troupes land onstage only after getting ready for any possibility. They practice and practice and practice so that no matter what happens, they are as ready as they can be. They practice thinking on their feet, flexibility, adaptability, and radical collaboration. Then the performers can trust both themselves and their colleagues to handle anything.

⚹ Improvisation works only after an enormous amount of thought and practice.

RAFAEL VINOLY

I've always practiced for everything, on my feet and aloud,

whether it is for a presentation, an important conversation, or the rough draft of a document. I've even read e-mails aloud before sending, to be sure the underlying spirit of the message is right.

So here's the real surprise: Most people in corporate environments don't want to practice. They're happy to think about something, or to write about it, but when it comes to practicing out loud and on their feet, they get shy. Very few industries outside of performance demand rehearsal, yet rehearsal is the most critical ingredient to success.

> ✳ Practice isn't the thing you do once
> you're good. It's the thing you do that
> makes you good.
>
> MALCOLM GLADWELL[1]

Our workshops can be a little uncomfortable for some people, but the workshops supply a safe place to practice, mess up, try again, try something new, and practice again. I encourage you to try the exercises in this book in a safe environment, to practice saying yes, and to get the behaviors into your body as much as into your mind. It's the most important part of making them a habit. Aristotle said, "We are what we repeatedly do. Excellence therefore is not an act, but a habit."

The second thing performers do is to celebrate big wins, small successes, getting through another day. The importance of celebrating what you've accomplished so far is a key to motivating, uplifting, and keeping everybody going.

In the early days of my company, I had to relearn that lesson myself. A member of my ensemble, Zoe Klopf-Switzer, and I were coming back from a very successful engagement. I made a point of thanking her for her great work, bought her a treat at the airport, and told her to enjoy some downtime. After I boarded the plane, however, I immediately opened up my laptop and started making a list of what I had to do next. My colleague shut my laptop and looked me in the eye.

"Raise your fists in the air," Zoe said, and I did. She instructed, "Now pump them up and down with me and say, 'Woo-hoo! We did it! We were great!'" After we celebrated and laughed, she plunked a fashion magazine on top of my closed laptop and ordered me a drink. Her last note to me was, "Would you please stop for a minute and remember to celebrate *yourself*?"

I realize that I often feel so driven, so responsible for the success of my company, that I forget to stop and celebrate. And if my team doesn't know whether I'm enjoying the work, whether I'm proud, they may not trust that I'm living the behaviors I so believe in.

Practice the behaviors. Celebrate even your tiny successes. All it takes is a little "Woo-hoo!" to yourself sometimes. You're doing great. Keep it up.

Notes

Introduction

Your Biggest Problem at Work and the Most Unexpected Solution

1. Peter Schwartz and Kevin Kelly, "The Relentless Contrarian," *Wired*, August 1996.

2. Daniel Goleman, *Emotional Intelligence: Why it Can Matter More than IQ* (New York: Bantam), 149.

3. Patricia Aburdene, *Megatrends 2010: The Rise of Conscious Capitalism* (Charlottesville, VA: Hampton Roads Publishing, 2005), xiv.

4. Booker T. Washington, *Up from Slavery: An Autobiography* (New York: The Country Life Press, 1900).

Chapter One

The First Secret of Improvisation: Yes! Space

1. Chip Heath and Dan Heath, *Switch: How to Change Things When Change Is Hard* (New York: Broadway Books, 2010).

2. George J. Firmage, ed., *E. E. Cummings: Complete Poems, 1904–1962* (New York: Liveright Publishing, 1978), 443.

3. Roger Fisher, William Ury, and Bruce Patton, *Getting to Yes: Negotiating Agreement without Giving In* (New York: Houghton Mifflin, 1991).

4. Dale Carnegie, *How to Win Friends and Influence People* (New York: Simon & Schuster, 1936).

5. Stephen Young, *MicroMessaging: Why Great Leadership Is beyond Words* (New York: McGraw-Hill, 2007).

6. Daniel Goleman, Richard Boyatzis, and Annie McKee, *Primal Leadership: Learning to Lead with Emotional Intelligence* (Boston: Harvard Business School Publishing, 2002).

7. Adrian Gostick and Chester Elton, *The Carrot Principle: How the Best Managers Use Recognition to Engage Their People, Retain Talent, and Accelerate Performance* (New York: Free Press, 2007).

8. Adapted from Karen Hough's Yes! Deck, available from improvedge.com.

Chapter Two
The Second Secret of Improvisation: Building Blocks

1. Stuart Brown and Christopher Vaughan, *Play: How It Shapes the Brain, Opens the Imagination, and Invigorates the Soul* (New York: Penguin, 2009), 29.

2. Ibid., 18.

3. Jim Collins, *Good to Great: Why Some Companies Make the Leap . . . and Others Don't* (New York: HarperCollins, 2001).

4. Adrian Gostick and Chester Elton, *The Carrot Principle: How the Best Managers Use Recognition to Engage Their People, Retain Talent, and Accelerate Performance* (New York: Free Press, 2007), 143–144.

5. Ben Fuchs, "Is Twitter Making You Stupid?," CNBC.com, August 26, 2009, http://www.cnbc.com/id/32569284/Is_Twitter_Making_You_Stupid.

6. Martin Wainwright, "Emails 'Pose Threat to IQ,'" Guardian.co.uk, April 22, 2005, http://www.guardian.co.uk/technology/2005/apr/22/money.workandcareers.

7. Adapted from Karen Hough's Yes! Deck, available from improvedge.com.

Chapter Three
The Third Secret of Improvisation: Team Equity

1. Jon R. Katzenbach and Douglas K. Smith, *The Wisdom of Teams: Creating the High-Performance Organization* (New York: Harper-Collins, 1993), 45.

2. James A. Belasco, *Teaching the Elephant to Dance: The Manager's Guide to Empowering Change* (New York: Plume, 1991).

3. From Roger von Oech's Creative Whack Pack (1992).

4. Roy D. Adler, *Women in the Executive Suite Correlate to High Profits* (Malibu, CA: Glass Ceiling Research Center, 2001), 2.

5. Adapted from Karen Hough's Yes! Deck, available from improvedge .com.

Chapter Four
The Fourth Secret of Improvisation: Oops to Eureka!

1. Vitruvius Pollio, *De Architectura*, bk. 9, introduction, para. 10.

2. www.cfy.org

3. Margaret Wheatley, *Leadership and the New Science: Discovering Order in a Chaotic World* (San Francisco: Berrett-Koehler Publishers, 1992), 19.

4. Adapted from Karen Hough's Yes! Deck, available from improvedge .com.

Conclusion
Practice. Then Celebrate!

1. Malcolm Gladwell, *Outliers: The Story of Success* (New York: Little, Brown, 2008), 42.

Acknowledgments

I first wish to thank my husband, Todd Majidzadeh, and my three children, Timothy, Kate, and Trey, for believing in me and supporting me. I love you. Thanks to Mom and Dad, for giving me every opportunity to grow and have a wonderful childhood. Thanks to my sister, Janice, for showing me courage in her lifetime. Thanks to my extended family.

I also must acknowledge the many people who had a part in editing, marketing, and creating this book. From the ImprovEdge ensemble: Jennifer Avery, Lorrie Diaz, Michael Everett-Lane, Christy Fryman, Signe Harriday, Artie Isaac, Erika Jackson, Zoe Klopf-Switzer, Jason Lorber, April Olt, Jamie Pachino, Chris Rabb, Michael Shepperd, Joel Showalter, Lisa Tennenbaum, David Thompson, Michelle Wilson, Ramon Ybarra. From Berrett-Koehler: Maria Jesus Aguilo, Charlotte Ashlock, Marina Cook, Michael Crowley, Kristen Frantz, Rachel Kador, Bonnie Kaufman, Shawn Kresal, Catherine Legronne, Zoe Mackey, Neil Maillet, David Marshall, Steve Piersanti (the visionary), Dianne Platner, Adryan Russ,

Katie Sheehan, Jeevan Sivasubramaniam, Cindy Ventrice, Johanna Vondeling, Rick Wilson. Thanks to those who were part of the story of this book: Coca-Cola Enterprises, Computers for Youth, Development Alternatives Inc., Frances Barney-Knutsen, Barbara Lauer, Legg Mason, NBBJ, Ologie, Professor Mike Useem.

Index

About the Author

Karen Hough was born an improviser. She didn't mind trying something new, she loved surprise and change, and she never saw a failure she didn't want to turn around. When she was a senior in high school, a classmate once asked her, "Aren't you afraid to go so far away to college?" It had never occurred to her to be afraid—only excited, and ready to jump in and play.

In college she was introduced to improvisational performance and her lifelong passion for improv began. She learned and deeply believed in the behaviors of positivity and radical collaboration that are necessary to improvisation. They became a way of life rather than just a performance technique.

Hough honed her skills with the Purple Crayon of Yale, trained with Second City of Chicago and the legendary Del

Close, and spent her first career as a successful improviser and actor onstage, on TV, and in film. She did over one hundred live productions.

But change is part of her DNA, so upon landing unexpectedly in New York during the Internet craze, she jumped into business. Untrained and unprepared, she relied on her improvisational skills to navigate the business landscape. She's the first to admit that 95 percent of her learning came from making mistakes—lots of mistakes! But she sure did learn quickly that way. It was an intense, wonderful, exhausting education in corporate America, and she discovered that business was her second passion. During the next six years, her persistence through difficulty paid off in unexpected success as a sales and marketing executive for the network engineering industry.

As time went on, an idea kept pricking her curiosity: could improvisational skills directly benefit businesspeople as they had benefited her? Luckily, the Wharton School agreed to let her and her colleagues try out their idea, which led to the birth of a business, ImprovEdge (www .ImprovEdge.com).

The toughest thing Hough remembers encountering in the early days was resentment. Even friends told her, "You can't have fun at work. This will never fly." There's nothing like a challenge to an improviser. Through continued university research, testing, and client partnerships, Hough introduced corporate clients to the improvisational skills of flexibility, radical collaboration, thinking on your feet, and turning mistakes into advantages. The results far exceeded everyone's expectations.

Since those first tests, Hough has worked with hundreds of clients, many in the Fortune 500, to develop their skills of leadership, change management, diversity and inclusion, sales, vision, presentation, and negotiation. She is the recipient of the Athena PowerLink award for outstanding female-owned businesses; is the author of the Yes! Deck; has been published in numerous magazines, blogs, and newsletters; and is on the board of Women for Economic Leadership and Development. She was honored as a Deloitte & Touche Wise Woman at their inaugural breakfast event in Columbus, Ohio, and she represented women entrepreneurs for the state of Ohio at the Saitama, Japan, Women's Contingent.

Hough is a graduate of Yale University and Université Paris-Sorbonne (Paris iv). She is deeply committed to volunteer activities and philanthropy. A portion of her company's profits each year go to support the Women's Fund of Central Ohio, Kiva, DonorsChoose, and cfy.org. Her volunteer activities include teaching improv classes for high school students in rural Kansas and confidence-building workshops for Chicago inner-city schoolchildren. She is a former board member of the Yale Whim 'n Rhythm Alumnae association and currently is a volunteer for Women for Economic Leadership and Development, the Yale Alumni Schools Committee, and the Yale Alumni Fund.

She resides in Columbus, Ohio, with her husband and three children. And as good as all this sounds, she'll tell you, "I still deal with roadblocks and make mistakes. You're just not trying hard enough, or risking enough, if you don't continue to hit bumps and learn along the way."

Berrett–Koehler
Publishers

Berrett-Koehler is an independent publisher dedicated to an ambitious mission: *Creating a World That Works for All*.

We believe that to truly create a better world, action is needed at all levels—individual, organizational, and societal. At the individual level, our publications help people align their lives with their values and with their aspirations for a better world. At the organizational level, our publications promote progressive leadership and management practices, socially responsible approaches to business, and humane and effective organizations. At the societal level, our publications advance social and economic justice, shared prosperity, sustainability, and new solutions to national and global issues.

A major theme of our publications is "Opening Up New Space." Berrett-Koehler titles challenge conventional thinking, introduce new ideas, and foster positive change. Their common quest is changing the underlying beliefs, mindsets, institutions, and structures that keep generating the same cycles of problems, no matter who our leaders are or what improvement programs we adopt.

We strive to practice what we preach—to operate our publishing company in line with the ideas in our books. At the core of our approach is stewardship, which we define as a deep sense of responsibility to administer the company for the benefit of all of our "stakeholder" groups: authors, customers, employees, investors, service providers, and the communities and environment around us.

We are grateful to the thousands of readers, authors, and other friends of the company who consider themselves to be part of the "BK Community." We hope that you, too, will join us in our mission.

A BK Business Book

This book is part of our BK Business series. BK Business titles pioneer new and progressive leadership and management practices in all types of public, private, and nonprofit organizations. They promote socially responsible approaches to business, innovative organizational change methods, and more humane and effective organizations.

Berrett–Koehler
Publishers

A community dedicated to creating
a world that works for all

Visit Our Website: www.bkconnection.com

Read book excerpts, see author videos and Internet movies, read
our authors' blogs, join discussion groups, download book apps, find
out about the BK Affiliate Network, browse subject-area libraries of
books, get special discounts, and more!

Subscribe to Our Free E-Newsletter, the *BK Communiqué*

Be the first to hear about new publications, special discount offers,
exclusive articles, news about bestsellers, and more! Get on the list
for our free e-newsletter by going to **www.bkconnection.com**.

Get Quantity Discounts

Berrett-Koehler books are available at quantity discounts for orders
of ten or more copies. Please call us toll-free at (800) 929-2929 or
email us at bkp.orders@aidcvt.com.

Join the BK Community

BKcommunity.com is a virtual meeting place where people from
around the world can engage with kindred spirits to create a world
that works for all. **BKcommunity.com** members may create their own
profiles, blog, start and participate in forums and discussion groups,
post photos and videos, answer surveys, announce and register for
upcoming events, and chat with others online in real time. Please join
the conversation!